Advance Praise for *Everything's a Two-Step but a Waltz: The Reluctant Texan Comes Home*

This story of resilience and rebirth, of recalibration and rediscovery, is a primer for all of us who find ourselves having to create a new life sometimes as in Morgan's case, virtually from the ground up and late in life. We journey with her as she wrestles with the magnitude of these changes, and previous ones, eventually discovering a totally unexpected new world of possibility in Texas, a place she believed she never wanted to see again. Morgan is a wonderful writer. She shares her pain with courageous honesty, while keeping herself and her readers sane through humor, poetry and song lyrics, and memorable tales of growing up as a military brat with two brothers, the first daughter on her father's side in several generations. The philosophical reflections woven into the two-step of her story telling are golden nuggets for anyone who must face their own demons and grow through seismic change to arrive, astonished, in a fulfilling new life.

~ Deirdre Taylor
Coach, Speaker, Writer, and "Diva"

Chick Morgan's story is her Dance About Life. She shares the perils of growing up and living as an adult in many diverse environments — San Antonio, Texas; Washington, D.C.; Germany; the Panama Canal Zone; New York City; Santa Barbara, California; Lubbock, Texas; and finally, the Hill Country artist community of Wimberley, Texas. Chick is a wonderful storyteller and demonstrates a keen sense of deprecating humor: "Everything's backwards in Texas. That's why I'm looking younger every day." Don't miss her story on firearms where she discovered the "two-step version" of a concealed handgun purse. Chick Morgan is an accomplished creative artist, singer songwriter, performer, and writer. This is definitely a Two-Step you will remember.

~ Patrick Cox, PhD.
Award-winning and nationally recognized Texas historian,
author, and sixth generation Texan

At first, I thought this was a book whose readership would be largely "the sisterhood." I was wrong. This book is for anyone with the following attributes: A person at a crossroads. A person who has begun to sense their own mortality. A person who appreciates the community they have. A person who wishes for a community but knows not how to go about it. Anyone who is going through or has been through major loss: of a parent, a relationship, a safe place they held dear, a job, or a career. Anyone who has been betrayed or disappointed. Men and women who have gone through one phase of life and are now contemplating what might be next for them. Your story of transformation and reinvention is relevant to all thinking people as we wrap our arms around inevitable change.

~ Jeff Connally
Former CEO, CMIT Solutions
Current Founder of the Appalachian Trail OGOWA Tribe
(Old Guys Out Walking Around)

I love your book. It dances so gracefully, so effortlessly, between comfortable soft flow and searing heartache, and back to the comfortable. The writing is so intimate it sparked my own memories. It needs to be a movie!

~ Susan Small
Attorney, Morgantown, West Virginia

EVERYTHING'S A TWO-STEP BUT A WALTZ

Mezcalita Press, LLC
Norman, Oklahoma

EVERYTHING'S A TWO-STEP BUT A WALTZ

The Reluctant Texan Comes Home

Chick Morgan

Table of Contents

Prologue

With a single step into the Sadako Peace Garden on the path of leafy mulch and discarded soft caramel-colored bark, the clean, sweet woody aroma of her 400 years worked its way deeply into my lungs and through the pores of my skin, infusing my brain with memories.

I began coming here as a student to find quiet and strength; later as a friend to a friend in need; often as a meditator early in the morning when the eucalyptus infusion was heaviest and laced with soft wisps of early morning fog.

One perfect Southern California blue skied morning I stood with my Beloved beneath the guardian Mother Overseer of me, the world, and 400 years of history, dreams, and sorrows and said, "I do," while we held each other's gazes and hands, inhaling the blessing of the tree. Dear friends surrounded us holding a branch – aromatic, sensual – the scent of deep connection among us and friendships shared.

Years later I sat on one of the stone benches in the quickening twilight of an early winter's evening, the wind sowing through the familiar branches of the huge tree. My ring felt cold in my gloveless hand as I reached for his. I placed it in his palm and closed his fingers around it. It had not been my choice for him to shatter my heart abruptly and irrevocably, but it was my choice to attempt leave-taking with a shred of grace in the finality, and under the watchful strength of the eucalyptus.

Who knows who she would tell this tale to over the next 400 years? But I would determine what the tale would be.

EVERYTHING'S A TWO-STEP BUT A WALTZ

The Reluctant Texan Comes Home

Double-Barreled Heartbreak

1 – Blindsided in the Line of Dance

I believe where we search, we are searched for.

~ David Wilcox

It is as wrong to ignore the possible as it is to deny the problem.

~ Dennis Salaby

I hadn't intended to throw up on the hotel bedspread. A few hours earlier I was sitting in the bar of a Red Lobster in San Antonio, after too many glasses of cheap red wine and too many tears. I texted my good friend from Connecticut who was vacationing in Jamaica.

"My mother died today," I wrote, "and that wasn't the worst thing that happened to me." The Red Lobster was no different than any Red Lobster off any loud, miserable interstate in the U.S., nothing that would later register in my mind's eye as regionally unique or particularly appealing. It was filled with nondescript, mainly overweight, mainly underdressed clientele looking for a cheap seafood combo plate with extra tartar sauce and a watery margarita or two to wash it down. At this late hour it was mostly businessmen staying, like me, at the Drury Inn across the parking lot next to the deafening interstate; or the occasional loner – man or woman – sitting with intentional space between them and the other customers, no need to talk to anyone except the bartender, or better, just point to their glass, the universal sign for "another."

After several days in the hospital, and two days in hospice critical care, my mother died. Here in Texas, we say "passed," or "went to be with the Lord," or "went to her reward," but never "died." But she did. She died.

Earlier that day my beloved husband of sixteen years called me from Santa Barbara where we were visiting for two months beginning our house hunt for our Big Transition from the east coast. He called to announce he was leaving me for a woman he'd met three weeks earlier in Santa Barbara. And no, she wasn't younger. Why is that the first thing everyone asks? I stood on my brother and sister-in-law's covered front porch in Wimberley, Texas, some part of my brain faintly registering the sight and delicate fragrance of the beautiful wisteria draping off the big Texas pine beams just inches away from me. I was seconds away from getting into their car for our trip to my parents' elegant, assisted living apartment in San Antonio. I was just hours away from when Hospice predicted, precisely on the money, she would die. I heard his words as they bounced between the cell phone and my ear, muffled, as if I were listening to them underwater.

Where were you last night? I couldn't get a hold of you on either your cell or the condo phone.

I was out with a woman I've wanted to know better. We had dinner at The Chart House and drinks afterwards at Fess's.

Till midnight? We never make it past 10:00!

If I only have 15 more years to live, I don't want them to be in this relationship.

I can't talk about this right now. I have to help my mother die.

I knew I could not and would not let anyone around me, my two brothers and their wives, or later, friends, know about this cataclysmic plot twist in my otherwise enviable, idyllic life. Part of me did not believe the last five minutes happened. All of me believed it could never happen to me, to us, the couple who had everything and seemed to know it; who were the center of our social, professional, and academic circles; who still lit up with pleasure when either walked into a room. The couple everyone wanted to be.

I knew everything had to be about my mother – not about me, and certainly not about him. I owed her that much after such a bumpy ride together throughout our lives. We were not close growing up. The emotional energy in my family was between me and Daddy. I was the first girl born on his side of the family in over 100 years. When I was young, my mother often went after me with a wooden spoon, a fly swatter, a switch, mean little weapons that would sting the backs of my legs, my calves, and leave small ugly welts. Later it would be hateful notes I would leave her on my pillow where she would be sure to find them as she (ironically, in hindsight) made my bed every morning, triggering a small spasm of guilt when I got home from school and eyed the tightly made-up bed.

Over the years those tensions eased and by the time I was an adult visiting my San Antonio hometown once or twice a year, I could companionably go shopping with her at the mall, give her a manicure and pedicure (her first). By then she had retreated more inward and lost any sense of self confidence or worth. She developed issues around her body. She would only go shopping for clothes with me, something I did that made my father grateful when I was in town. Sometimes she and I would just sit and chat while we watched Lawrence Welk, The Gaither Family Hour, or the Golf Channel, especially when Tiger Woods was playing and during those years that was almost all the time. We were not close, but we had made an easy peace. Now, standing on that peaceful Texas Hill Country porch, I knew that to get through not just the one ordeal of her death later that afternoon, but also the anguishing news of my husband's treachery, I had to draw on all my fortitude and focus and, mostly, God help me, my legendary Texas Grit. And I had to do it alone.

Later that night, sitting at the tacky bar in that tacky restaurant, I knocked back cheap cabernet glass after glass. I knew I needed to talk to my best friend. I texted, and the return text was immediate: "Don't do anything. Don't go anywhere. I am calling you now." After a few seconds the call from Jamaica came and I sat there for an hour sobbing and drinking and wailing with no one else around but the nervous looking bartender. Wailing. For whom? My mother? Myself? I didn't know, didn't care, and it didn't matter. His words were echoing in my mind:

If I only have fifteen more years…Not with you…If I only have…If only…

The few other late-night customers that had been at the Red Lobster bar quietly settled up with the bartender and made their exit. I was such a nasty, noisy, snotty mess I had cleared the room. I would have left as well, but I was bolted to the wooden barstool, clutching my purse like a sinking ship's life preserver to make sure it didn't touch the dirty, napkin strewn floor. It was just me, the bartender now keeping a cautious distance, and my "lifeline call a friend" friend. Wine slopped out of one of the chugged glasses and worked its way up from the sticky, grimy counter to the cuff of my expensive ivory silk blouse, spreading like an oozing blood stain.

Somehow I got back to my hotel room. I have no recollection
of paying the bill, leaving the bar, or stumbling back across the
parking lot in the dark. I woke up in my clothes lying on the
bed, sick from all the drinking, feeling the cheap wine from the
night before beginning its inevitable journey up and out. I
cleaned up the room as best I could, showered a long time
under needles of piping hot water, made a big pot of hotel
room faux Starbucks coffee, disappointingly weak, of course. I
dressed and went to the hotel lobby to meet up with my brother
and sister-in-law staying there as well. As far as I know, they,
nor anyone else, ever knew what happened the day before and
what I was dealing with aside from my mother's death. That's
the way I wanted it.

Earlier the day before, the funeral home workers left with my
mother's shrouded body riding the hospital bed on wheels one
last time. She had ridden down the hallway sitting up and waving to everyone like the Queen of Sheba, clearly happy to be
returning to her apartment after a couple days in the hospital.
We all knew she was returning to hospice, but for the moment,
she was enjoying the attention and so were all of us. Now, I
went upstairs to Mother and Daddy's apartment. I needed to
see for myself she was gone.

I went into the bathroom off their bedroom. There on the sink
counter, where she'd left them just a few days before being
unexpectedly admitted to the hospital, were her lipstick and
blush, both Estee Lauder products she enjoyed for many years
and my sister-in-law kept well and lovingly supplied for her.
They were the same colors she'd worn the last decade of her life
– Cocoa Rose lipstick and Fresh Plum powder blush. I picked
up the lipstick and twisted the tube until the color came up on

its stalk, noticing the distinct curvature hollowed out on the lipstick, unique to her, as is every woman's. Perhaps that specific indentation on a specific woman's lipstick might be better than the traditional fingerprint or dental records we typically used for identification. On an impulse I ran it along my lower lip. The indentation fit perfectly. Of course it would. We were so much alike physically. Similar coloring, facial structure, hands, and now, irrefutably, our lips. As I've aged, I've come to recognize an unexpected occasional tone of voice, a fidget of the hands in the way we would each chat at the dinner table in our after-dinner family confabs, folding and refolding a cloth napkin, a set of the jaw when I was displeased with something but too angry or uncomfortable to say something. In those moments, I didn't feel I *looked like* my mother, which I do and more so as I've aged, but *felt like* her, as if there were some plane of reality in which we co-existed as the same person. So many years I tried to put distance between us, physically and emotionally, and now here it was, my final physical contact with her after she's gone. The lipstick and blush were some of the last physical things she touched and had touched her. Now they were touching me. We were, in the end, so much alike, but this revelation was unexpected and hit me with an emotional wallop I hadn't seen coming.

I stumbled through the next few days in a daze confirming funeral arrangements and wrestling with legal details. Daddy, bereft and confused, wandered in and out of this new reality in his rapidly increasing dementia.

"Where's Mom? Oh, I remember! She's out shopping with her girlfriends." She did not have girlfriends and she never shopped, never really had except when I was along with her on one of my visits. Most of her funeral details were planned. Daddy was a retired thirty-year full colonel in the Army so planning and having things buttoned up were important and a way of life in our lives, then, as we grew up, and now. Years earlier, on the day they went to the funeral home to pick out their caskets, my mother announced in an uncharacteristically cheery fashion that she had selected "a pretty pink satin one," but also insisted adamantly she did *not* want an open coffin. "I don't want anyone looking at me when I'm dead!" For years I wondered at the absurdity of that statement until I connected it with the deep southern roots of her south Virginia tobacco farm childhood not far from the mountains of Appalachia, forty miles from Appomattox. It was an odd combination of rural superstitious beliefs and her adamant insistence about never being the center of attention. Ever. Mom had also met with the catering staff of their home, the Army Residence Community (The ARC) years earlier and planned the menu for her reception: chicken fingers, "those nice little nuts," mints, and I don't remember what else, frankly. I was grateful it was planned and planned by her. A fitting finale for someone who had so little control over her life when she was alive.

They were married 74 years. During her brief hospital stay he never left her side or let go of her hand or stopped saying, "I love you," or "you are a beautiful woman," or "you've been a wonderful wife and the best thing that ever happened to me." He'd adored her their whole lives although with varying degrees of success in showing it.

Part of the process of any parent's passing, particularly for the only daughter, is going through the family albums – "Take what you want, please!" "Please look through these photos!" And I did. Boxes and boxes of them, surprisingly, many of Mother and Daddy and their families I had not seen before, some distant relatives I recognized, most I didn't, some with hand-written comments and names on the backs, most without.

I found myself enchanted with the photos of my mother when she was young, even before she met Daddy. I have her high school annual of her last year, her dark hair coiffed with waves and draped with the satin drape all the young women wore for their photo. She looked shy, but happy. A sweet, uncomplicated smile. In later photos of her and Daddy in their early years I see her as a young woman – photos capturing her in mid-surprise, full throated laugh, full facial smile, probably before life got so hard with three kids and a husband in the military and the moving around and her having to hold things together for months sometimes, or a year when Daddy was in Korea, or Language School in Monterrey, California.

When I thought of my mother as an adult, which is how I remembered her until I spent hours with the old photographs, I thought of her as introverted, not especially joyous – caring absolutely, but not joyous. I never had a sense of who she was as a woman – young, middle-aged, old – or what she thought about her life. As years went by, her emotional bandwidth for expressing happiness or joy of any shade seemed to diminish. I had no messy unfinished business or unresolved issues with her by that time, so when she died, I could hold her hand and tell her I loved her and wish her a sweet and gentle passing.

The gradual shift in affection between my parents over the years was not something I was privy to. They still shared many loving moments and laughter and humor, reminiscences of their life together, their embarrassingly unabashed love, enjoyment, and pride in their grown children. The corresponding attempts over the years by my father to buy her gifts for each Mother's Day, birthday, Christmas, or Valentine's Day felt charged with anxiety. I was enlisted on my trips home to accompany Daddy on gift buying excursions, gifts which usually elicited a polite nod and patented, "Oh, thank you," from my mother, but seldom more. The tension in these exchanges became palpable. He, anxious to please her. She, quietly withholding that pleasure. Despite that, contrasting the image of my grieving father expressing his love non-stop to his dying wife, I began replaying the brief morning conversation with my own husband from a few days earlier, disturbingly on auto replay in my head.

Where were you last night?

I was out with a woman I've wanted to get to know better…If I only have fifteen more years…

Where on earth had he come up with *that* number, I remember thinking. I called my husband later that day after my mother died and gave him the news. "I need you to get to San Antonio as quickly as you can. I need you."

"I'll only come if you swear you won't demonize me to everyone." *That* was his concern? "Of course, I won't *demonize* you," I spat. "This isn't about you."

Years later I wonder why I felt the need to protect him and collude in that absurd narcissistic demand. I believe it was me I was trying to protect, maybe because letting others in on that awful news would wreak havoc on my family's story line about us because, as my father had told me at least a hundred times, "After all these years, Honey, you finally found a winner." Damning with faint praise as the saying goes. The third time's the charm and all that. Given my dismal track record with marriage and divorce, not unwarranted. Maybe on some level I already suspected that his sudden jumping ship was my fault, some lack in me, that I deserved to be blindsided. Many more years later I realize there is no such thing, really, as being totally blindsided. The silent and not so silent clues were there, bobbing quietly like a cork on a quiet lake or even, occasionally, surfacing boldly like a trout, but ignored, overlooked, stuffed hurriedly into some corner of my heart, somewhere I believed was safe even from myself.

After several days of memorial service and burial details I faced the worst journey of all, back to Santa Barbara, not back to Connecticut where we lived in our small, Idyllic Cottage Antique Barn we'd rented near the water a year before to downsize from our large, architecturally significant dream home we'd lived in for 13 years. The dream house in the bucolic Connecticut countryside was designed by Yann Weymouth, Managing Architect for I.M. Pei. We walked in and it im-mediately triggered the fantasy of my husband who was intent on leaving his life and persona as the hot shot New York writer and becoming the genteel, gracefully aging Connecticut country gentleman writer. The house was a residential plaything the architect constructed between projects such as the East Wing of the National Gallery and the Pyramid at The Louvre. He'd toyed with the idea for years – building an international Bau-haus style contemporary box house inside of and suspended from a vintage 150-year-old barn. It was a dream house, a forever house. But we had sold it a year earlier and downsized to move on to the much-anticipated next stage of our lives – the Santa Barbara stage – which we'd planned for several years.

Now I had to fly back to Santa Barbara, get my things from the cramped, pedestrian two-bedroom two-bath condo we'd rented for two months, and fly home as soon as possible, pack my things, get out of the Idyllic Cottage Antique Barn and do something – anything - but stay in that cottage. It was Ready Fire Aim. I had no plan A, no Plan B, or C. I wallowed in the confusion and, truthfully, the righteousness and self-justification of being totally blindsided, my anger cowering at the feet of disbelief.

If I only have…If only…

I had no immediate cash flow as my successful global consulting business of twenty-five years had bottomed out during the 2008-2009 economic crash. We had assets but I had no access to them or independent support. Proposal after proposal, project after project I'd been offered over the past several years, all solid looking at the time, evaporated. Long before "ghosting" became a popular cultural term I was sharing my life with ghosts everywhere. Three contracted years with a French aviation company evaporated when the CEO, my client, died unexpectedly. A multi-year executive education contract with a leading business school disappeared with a change in leadership. One after another of these opportunities, once gleaming with professional potential and fat profit, evaporated. I had owned my international consulting business for many years and was all too familiar with the vagaries of this kind of work, the ephemeral come and go nature of it, but never all at once and in such a short period of time as this. The fear I could clearly figure out. The pain was still a muddled-up mystery. For my mother? For him? For the marriage? It didn't matter. It was all pain, and it felt the same. The pain didn't discriminate. It didn't play favorites or make a priority list as my professional self was inclined to do. Whatever the source, its laser beam focus was relentlessly, mercilessly drilling a hole into me deeper and deeper.

In desperation, I grasped onto a straw of an idea, a bad idea, but at least an idea: since Santa Barbara was where we'd been heading as a couple, then Santa Barbara was where I was going to go. Find a job, any job, find a cheap apartment to rent (a unicorn in Santa Barbara), pack up my car and drive across the country. Move. Just keep moving. Don't sit still. Because when I sat still all I could do was heave and moan and tumble into the fiery crater of fear, the flames burning me alive. Fear gripped me from the moment I woke, whether at 2:00 a.m., 4:00 a.m., or just before dawn. My heart pounded like it was coming right out of my chest. My breath was hot and ragged. I managed to get prescriptions for both anxiety and insomnia from my parents' doctor at The ARC. The doctor assumed the request was to help get me through the stress of my mother's death and my father's dementia, which was true, but just barely.

Aided by the lovely drugs which slowed down my racing mind and heart enough at times to allow me to think a little more clearly, the first shift in my thinking occurred on my flight to Connecticut back from Santa Barbara where I'd packed up my things from the condo. The linen jackets and dresses I reveled wearing there in January and February were coming back with me. Strappy sandals and cute short suede boots, too. Things I could only dream of wearing again in several more months back in Connecticut. Books that I thought I might need and could ship later I took to our small storage unit in Santa Barbara. It was the cases of wine collected at various well-known wineries in California's beautiful wine rich central coastal countryside I resented packing away the most and leaving in the storage unit. It killed me to know he and what's-her-name would be enjoying them with intimate dinners, cooked in her (in his words to our good friend Jack) "utterly fabulous house," an award winning multi-million dollar solar powered perfectly and painstakingly remodeled California Craftsman Cottage with an ocean view from every room, and with a "kitchen he couldn't stop talking about…." It was an improvement, for sure, over the small two-bedroom condo we'd rented with its tiny two-butt size kitchen with a round dinette table and four chairs, not unlike what we would most likely find to live in for a while when we moved to Santa Barbara.

As I'd been reminded by him several months earlier, my "inability to generate income has become corrosive to our relationship." My fear and inner knowing had quickly filed that one far away and deep in my consciousness, only to be resurrected and hauled out months later when the happy couple were spotted in the VIP Donor box of one of Santa Barbara's many upscale philanthropic high dollar fundraising events. No. She wasn't younger. But she did have others assets.

Later that year, months and miles away from the wrenching devastation of those early days, I recalled a quote I'd read in an essay by P. J. O'Rourke, the political satirist and journalist, about the fall of the Soviet Union in 1989. I had been working in the Soviet Union at the time and the satellite Communist countries, so it caught my attention:

> *In the end we beat them with Levi 501 jeans. Seventy-two years of communist indoctrination and propaganda were drowned out by a three- ounce Sony Walkman. A huge totalitarian system…has been brought to its knees because nobody wanted to wear Bulgarian shoes.*

Maybe, I reasoned from hindsight, the thought of living in a downsized two-bedroom condo with a postage-stamp sized kitchen and dinette set was just more than he could realistically stomach – his equivalent of Bulgarian shoes.

On the flight over the Grand Canyon and red rocks of Utah, the green farmlands of the Midwest and, finally, the bays and waterways and shorelines of the Atlantic, we approached

LaGuardia Airport on the descent back to the East Coast, and I heard something. Maybe an angel whispered. Who knows? Don't judge. But a voice said, "You are consumed with all you've lost – your marriage, your mother, your home, your income, your career, the life you loved and anticipated having through your dying days. But what is still here, in front of you, right this minute?" It wasn't a priority list I made, or a pros and cons table.

I made sure my seat belt was buckled, my seat and tray table were in their righteous upright position, my carry-on stowed, more accurately stuffed, beneath my seat. I scribbled a surprisingly short list on a smudged crumpled paper beverage coaster I found under my foot:

- I have my immediate family, few as they are, but they are mighty
- I have amazing friends in many places nurtured over many years
- I have the freedom now to do anything I want (if I can figure out how to do it)

Everything changed. I was determined to focus on the strong and good and positive things in my life while I stumbled along from one agonizing sleepless night and day into another, all the while drinking too much wine. (One thing at a time.) As I thought about packing my car in Connecticut and rushing back to Santa Barbara to cobble together a life in a place full of daily reminders of what could have been, one question rumbled through my brain like Cole Porter's Beat Beat Beat of the tom tom, and the Tick Tick Tock of the stately clock, and the Drip Drip Drip of the raindrop. If I didn't do *that,* what could I do? Well, I could think about moving to another small attractive community where I also have friends. That could be exciting.

My work and career, which I hoped would ultimately pick up again at some point, were not geographically dependent.

And…if I didn't do *that,* what could I do? The answer came to me. I could travel and see friends I haven't seen in a while and perhaps spend the kind of time together that the everyday patterns of lives and living make difficult – more than dinner at an academic conference, a glass of wine at the airport when traveling through town, a brief weekend in each other's home if we were so lucky. My stepchildren, (or "children of affection" which is the language we always used), were out of college and on their own. Our ancient, infirmed, three-legged cat had conveniently died a few days before our ill-fated Santa Barbara trip. A foreshadowing perhaps?

Back in Connecticut I sat with that question as I moved my clothes, books, and computers – again – this time out of the Idyllic Antique Cottage Barn and into a suite of rooms in which I had been offered sanctuary. My new sanctuary was in the home of the same friend I called from the miserable Red Lobster that first awful night. I was offered safe haven, a landing field, and a mailing address, something I'd never given any thought to whatsoever, from which I could take the time to figure out what I might do, what I could do, what was now possible.

Those first few months, I was back and forth to San Antonio, first to bury my mother several weeks after her death. As a military wife she was to be buried in Fort Sam Houston National Cemetery. It was during a peak time of one of the middle east wars and too many soldiers, as in every war, were dying and being buried in the national cemeteries. The ceme-teries were busy. She had to wait her turn. It was a strange holding period, but Mom wouldn't have been bothered by that.

She was an Army wife and used to waiting for all kinds of
things, things like Daddy moving to the top of the next
promotion list, the hamburger at the commissary to drop a few
cents a pound, for news of the next assignment and relocation.
I like to think she was enjoying the beautiful pink silk lined
coffin in that interim, and, finally, some long overdue and much
deserved time to herself.

My husband, or His Nibs[1] as I began to think of him, and I flew
in for Mom's memorial service and burial on separate flights,
which was not unusual over the years given our various busy
travel schedules. He, of course, was flying in from Santa
Barbara, and I was flying in from Connecticut. Together we
went through all the motions with family. No one knew our
situation. I even sang my mother's favorite hymn at her service,
"The Love of God." In a rare burst of sharing something
personal, she'd once told me how much she loved that hymn. I
had sung it once at the ARC in the Sunday Chapel service while
visiting. She sat about ten rows from the front of the Chapel
instead of in the first pew with my father and me, insisting, as
usual, she didn't want anyone looking at her. I began the hymn
that Sunday morning at the Chapel service and watched the
dawn of recognition on her face. I watched a slow paralysis take
over with the unexpected emotional intimacy it implied between
us. She never mentioned it then or ever.

His Nibs showed up at the funeral service and the cemetery
burial, his usual charming, elegant, socially pitch perfect self
with my family and friends, and even me. He reminded me of
Matt Damon in the movie *The Talented Mr. Ripley,* morphing
effortlessly to meet the requirements of whatever social situation presented. No one knew what was happening between us,
other than my good friend in Connecticut. No one. I should
have won an Oscar.

Shortly after the service and burial I wrote a note to immediate family members and my closest circle of friends about the chaos of the last few weeks. One friend compared the jolting news about The Perfect Couple and The Couple Everyone Wanted to Be to "the earth falling off its axis." Now the grief and exploration and journey and quest for first, survival, and ultimately my next stage of life, began in earnest. In the back of my mind I angrily ranted, "I am too damn old for this – again! How many times am I going to have to do this in my one stellar lifetime?" Clearly, at least three.

Thank God, neither my dead mother nor my poor demented daddy ever had to experience the treachery and callousness of my husband's actions. Even though he was a bona fide member of the East Coast liberal intelligentsia clan, a combination of qualities they despised, they both adored him, and truly believed he'd hung that big 'ol Texas moon and all those "stars at night so big and bright." Another conquest by Mr. Ripley, one of many I'd see him maneuver over the years, while privately admitting disdain for them, my family, and all things Texas.

I made my multiple trips to Texas over the next few weeks in the newly christened Year of The Great Shitstorm to be with Daddy. I didn't have a plan other than to be with Daddy frequently and check in with my family there. On those trips I stayed in my brother and sister-in-law's home in Wimberley, a haven of love, peace, art, and inimitable caring in the beautiful Texas Hill Country between Austin and San Antonio.

Most people who have never been to Texas, or that part of Texas, find it hard to believe Texas has hills, or such lush rolling landscape, oak trees, gorgeous wildflowers and now, dozens of increasingly well-regarded wineries with their rolling hillside vineyards. It's still pretty much "our secret," entre nous, so I am trusting you not to spread the word. My good friend Jack, a cultured New York and European self-proclaimed foodie, wine snob, and chef, on one spectacularly beautiful, blue-skied January day overlooking the vineyards of a favorite winery, declared the area "an undiscovered Sonoma" while we sipped a respectable Viognier.

The plan to see friends anywhere and everywhere and spend time with them was a liberating and welcome prospect. These friends had invited us for years to their homes; a chateau in the Alps, a 5000-acre sheep ranch in the rolling hills of western Colorado, a beautiful three-bedroom three-bath beachfront condo on the Outer Banks. The invitations were always greeted with some version of "We'd love to but we just don't have the time." "We'd love to, but my husband's writing and teaching and consulting schedule just won't permit it." The truth was my husband had no interest in going to "that place," being with "those friends," or whatever it was, so I was left to cover our social tracks with gracious demurring and my impeccable Texas bred warmth and social skills. Over years, the invitations became less frequent and eventually stopped. But now I could say yes. And I did. Yes, and yes and yes.

Who doesn't like a road trip? It was rumored in my family that as I slid down the birth canal that sunny June day and glided into the waiting arms of the pediatric nurse, she distinctly heard something that sounded gleefully gurgled like, "Oooooo! Road Trip!" My first. I was hooked. I have no way to corroborate that, but I admit it feels true.

I quelled the chronic small waves of dis-ease about spending time in Texas even for the most honorable and worthy reasons such as I had. As an adult I had managed to play up my roots there as ironic so no one in my non-Texas life would take my intermittent returns seriously. I was a captive as a child, hijacked as all children are at their parents' whims, to take me whatever place we were destined to live next. I couldn't be responsible for those years.

"Can you really imagine me there long term?" Of course, they couldn't. I was away for more than forty years. Texas felt more alien, less comfortable, less interesting with every husband, career move, and experience. I deeply preferred my new life. Unfortunately, it was the one I'd just lost.

I had been gone a long time. During that time I had collected an impressive collection of cowboy boots including my Lucchese ostrich boots and my red calf Tony Lamas. The collection was an ironic signature. I stood out from the average New Yorker, another move to make myself memorable. It worked. His Nibs liked to tell the story that he was not entirely convinced I had decided to move in with him until one day he noticed all my boots were in our closet. The way I let him know I was fully out of our home and moving on was to tell him, "Don't worry. You're safe now. My boots are gone."

I knew almost nothing about Texas dancing. My first Texas Two-Step partner and teacher was my late father-in-law, the father of my first husband, West Point Starter Husband, the only father-in-law I ever had. My father-in-law was a multi-generation Texan, professional rodeo calf roper turned successful high end western wear and western art entrepreneur. I know now I was in love with West Point Starter Husband's family, especially his dad. And who wouldn't be? Bill was tall, lanky, impeccably dressed in elegant western style. He wore his hat, boots, and custom-made western shirts and suits looking like The Marlborough Man, which he was mistaken for one day we were together on a New York City sidewalk. Wry, smart, gentleman to his core, as true as the way is North. On a memorable night in a hot West Texas dance hall on a family outing, Father-in-Law swung me around the dance hall in the line of dance, keeping me upright and in rhythm. Quick-quick, slow-slow, moving together. I was aware of the admiring looks from the sidelines. Quick-quick, slow-slow. In Texas two-stepping, like many other dances, you and your partner dance together with no eye contact, looking out across your partner's shoulder to some "soft" spot in the distance as you go around together in the line of dance. This only works because every other part of your bodies is in tune, cueing off each other, feeling the infinitesimal movements that keep you moving together around the dance hall in the same counterclockwise direction with all the other dancers. Slow-slow, quick-quick. Just like life. Just like the ebb and flow of a well-tuned long-term relationship. And just what His Nibs and I were not able to accomplish. We never quite caught the rhythm for the line of dance – not that his utter disdain and sneering lip curl at the very mention of Texas or anything about it (one of the many things we had in common) would have allowed him to try.

In hindsight, I believe it was my mother who did the blind-siding. My no drama mama. She wasn't supposed to die, at least not then. In a song I wrote about her years later I sang, "I knew that she loved me but that's all that I knew."[2] In the end that was enough. She was the strong one. The practical one. Her mind and body were ninety-one years old. She was lucid in her thoughts and clear as a bell in her speech, but I believe she'd just had enough of all of it. Holding her hand as she died, I suddenly *knew*. Dealing with Daddy, his forgetfulness, his repetition of questions, his hearing loss, was all too hard for her at the end of the line like this. Who could blame her? She'd always been short on compassion and dealing with Daddy's frustrations and difficulties emptied what little was left in the reserve tank. She was tired. And who wouldn't be? Who would have guessed she was the one with enough (God help me I have to say it) *grit* to just quit and pull the plug. You go, Mom. In the end it was easier really. Just as it was for me when my husband just quit and pulled the plug on our marriage in one yank instead of dragging unhappiness out for years, only to result in the same ending. Slow-slow. Quick-quick.

Over the years I have reluctantly revised my belief about that day and being blindsided. He did tell me. In the way he stopped holding my hand as we crossed a street or walked a beach. In the way he set up a separate office in the neighborhood of our Idyllic Cottage Antique Barn, rather than contently sharing close quarters and workspaces for days or weeks on end as we had in the big house. The way he would briskly walk ahead of me on our morning beach walks so he was twenty yards ahead before I knew it. The way he just quit cooking at home. Most pointedly, during the months he was seeking treatment for "low testosterone," whatever that's supposed to mean, I jokingly said, "There's a reason the 'little blue pill' is a billion-dollar industry," to which he replied, "Yes, but it can't manufacture desire." Now I replay those conversations over in my mind and think, "Ouch. Double ouch." But at the time I let them slide by, giving them no traction or purchase in my heart or mind, afraid to follow them someplace I suspected they were going, but did not want to follow. In hindsight it was especially confusing since only a few months before, when I'd asked if he wanted me to come along on some errands, he'd stated, "Everything's better when you're along."

There is a scene in the movie *Eat Pray Love* where Julia Roberts looks at the storage unit she's just loaded with her remaining belongings, commenting on the fact her whole life fits in a twelve-foot square box. The storage unit manager replies how often people say that and "most people never come back for their whole life." My life fit into one-third of a POD container.

Adventures and explorations were before me in the months ahead. Travel. Friends. Writing. Honest conversations. Soul searching. Fear infused nights. The hard work of building a life again. Where it would all end up I didn't want to think about yet. I was almost sixty-four years old and starting over for a third time with no one to need me or feed me. Again. What would the Beatles have made of that? Strike Three. I knew wherever "this" was or whatever "this life" was going to be, it was not going to be in Texas. Knowing that, by itself, was a relief.

My suitcase lay open and before I zipped it, I folded my ivory silk blouse, restored from its Red Lobster encounter, and placed it on top. It was time to move on, get out there, and figure out some new steps, one step at a time, knowing it would probably be slow-slow at first, and maybe for a long time.

The Ones You Don't See Coming

Music and Lyrics by Shelley King
©2019 Lemonade Records
2008 Official State Musician of Texas

Hidden from the radar in the still of the night
Left total devastation in the morning light
Rain wrapped tornado, invisible storm
Never saw it coming. No sirens to warn.

The worst are the ones you don't see coming
They sneak up on you when your guitar's strumming
They knock you to your knees while your drum is drumming
Watch out for the ones you don't see coming
Watch out for the ones you don't see coming.

Under cover and disguised in a curtain of rain
Waiting for the moment to inflict its pain
You head straight into the darkness with no fear or doubt
Then it chews you up and spits you out

Chorus

You can't calm something like this,
no way to fight, no way to resist.
How can you save the love you've missed
after the winds have blown?

You gotta learn to feel it, you gotta ride the wind
Knowing where you're going, knowing where you've been
Oh it won't make a difference, when it's time, it's time
Things are gonna change, on that you can rely.

2 – Redemption at the Dump

What…a…dump!

~ Betty Davis
in the film *Beyond the Forest*, 1949

I'm not in the business of forgiveness. That's God's turf. When The Great Shitstorm hit I spent too much precious life force looking for answers when there weren't any for me. For all I can tell, not for him, either. I knew, though, I would have to wrestle with the question of rebalance in my life, the baby steps of moving on, or getting past what I'd never get over. I decided to let the unanswerable question of "why" lie and focus on making a new life. But thinking about the past few months I recalled the specific incident that triggered my need to stop floundering and move on.

It started with some memories of Ireland, a place of deep spirituality and creative insight for me, a place I have been to dozens of times.

Some places look just like they're supposed to look, or at least the way my imagination demands they look. Ireland is one of those places. Reliably, perfectly, relentlessly green, stonewalled and sheeped at every turn of a winding lane. New York City is one of those places. Sky scraped, car horned, and shoulder to shoulder thronged with rushing people. Connecticut is one of those places. Rocky beached, colonial homed, maple tree redded, winding roads lined with ancient looking stone walls along glittering reservoirs, ponds, and fly fishing rivers.

That's exactly how Fairfield County, Connecticut greeted us when His Nibs and I began scouting the area as a potential homesite for our new life. He became familiar with the thickly wooded landscape when visiting his college roommate and his roommate's parents who lived there.

The college he attended in upstate New York was one of the "small ivys" always teetering on broader recognition, one which hits no one's screen until someone, somewhere, refers to it out of the blue. His roommate's father was a Broadway producer with several well-regarded hits to his credit, as well as the corresponding equalizing humility-inducing flops.

His roommate's parents lived in a 60s contemporary home in one of the multi-acred, gladed lake properties in New Canaan. His Nibs attended Broadway openings with his roommate and family, then waited with them at the legendary Sardi's restaurant for the reviews, a storied tradition that perfectly aligned with his self-ascribed desired public persona as "To The Manor Born." He never was, unfortunately, born to any manor, but that never stopped him from acting the part, resulting in presenting as if he were. His middle manager engineer father and his stay-at-home-turned-receptionist mother, only wanted to hit the respected flats of the middle-class, which they did. The longing for upward mobility quietly flared from his mother like a flare from the natural gas pipelines of the West Texas oil plains casting a shadow of dis-ease in the family.

I don't recall being in that part of Connecticut before our scouting trips but listening to the honey-coated yearning in his voice to be a part of that class and culture on his own terms, to be regarded as a legitimate member of the New York writer

intelligentsia and upper-class Broadway world that it represented, I gave in to his desire to find a place that suited us.

Fairfield County was beautiful and looked the part of quiet old
money. A movie location scout would have chosen it to house a
well-heeled sophisticated East Coast intellectual. His Nibs was
the star of that theoretical movie and had found his perfect set.
It was time to move on from his previous period of twenty
years living in his co-op in the West Village of New York,
intellectual/writer about town, bachelor until he was snagged
just as he turned forty. The West Village co-op was purchased
with the royalties from his successful first book, "a Book of the
Month Club Alternate Selection" as he was fond of reminding
everyone. It was time to leave New York City, he insisted, but
he wanted to be close enough to spend time with his young
daughter still living in New York with her mother.

I was living happily in New England in central Vermont in a
picturesque village, in an idyllic log home sitting on seven acres
with a half-acre pond four miles up a dirt road backing up
against a state forest. My work took me around the world. I split
my time with a shared apartment on Riverside Drive on the
Upper West Side. A small office for my international consulting
practice was situated next door to the country store in the small
Vermont town, consisting of three rooms overlooking the perfect Main Street. The office suited me well until one day, my
client from Singapore on the other end of our call said, puzzled,
"What is that horrible noise? I can barely hear you!" I had left
the window in my main office open that day, inviting in the
warm breeze of a mid-summer day.

"Oh, that's the band from our elementary school practicing
marching for the Fourth of July Parade. They're great, aren't
they?" Truth was, they were not. I was not interested in making

a change and moving again to be closer to New York full-time when we got together, but he would not consider living in such a rural backwater place.

We found a charming house to rent in Fairfield County. It was on a well-treed acre, down a short winding lane and within earshot of a noisy brook. Discrete two-acre-plus parcels with restored historic colonials and tasteful mid-century homes dotted the road. Think Phillip Johnson's Glass House; the 70s film classic *The Ice Storm*. Think Burt Lancaster in the film *The Swimmer,* making his way from pool to pool across our very neighborhood. Everything about Fairfield County spoke of quiet taste and a haven for artists, *New Yorker* writers, illustrators, and editors, as well as famous actors and television personalities. Paul Newman and Joanne Woodward's farm estate was a few miles towards town. Robert Redford, Jose Feliciano, and Lester Holt lived low-key lives around one corner or another. No one, of course, would ever dream of saying anything to Paul Newman in the gym of the local Y, all of us sweating together in preferred mutual anonymity.

After a couple of years His Nibs and I acquired our own architecturally significant homestead. It was a stunning Bauhaus box contemporary suspended inside an 1840's Connecticut onion barn. The architect was an international household name who amused himself one summer by designing and building "a new house in an old barn," a quirky aspiration he'd apparently harbored for years according to articles in *Architectural Digest* and *Women's Day.* The house sat on a hillside overlooking three acres tumbling down with wildflowers, thistle, meadow grasses and maples of many kinds. All the bounty was enjoyed by the inhabiting wild turkeys, foxes, and birds. It was paradise. We were happy. It was no longer solely his longing and manifested yearning for a different life. I shared his obsession.

Daily I made the mental contrast between this picture book
setting and the dusty, flat, tract-filled developments of Texas.
His Nibs had often expressed gratitude for the people living in
Texas, and places like it, such as his own Midwest hometown.
"If they are living there," he reasoned, "they are not living
where we want to live." Over time I'd become as disdainful of
everything but manors and refined luxury as he was. The
longing reeked off of both of us. I was surprised and amused
how often I would hear the same response from people in
Texas when I was visiting and they asked where I lived.

"Oh, Connecticut!" was the usual gushing comment. "That's so
beautiful! I've never been there of course, but I know it's just
beautiful!"

The Manor Born required work, the reason we were able to
acquire it in the intentionally prohibitively expensive neighborhood. His Nibs always wanted to be identified with the finer
things of life, but he wanted to acquire those things at the
lowest cost possible. His mantra was to buy everything –
clothes, furniture, cars – at "the bottom of the high" or "the top
of the low." This was never more evident than in the remodel-
ing and furnishing of our exquisite dream house.

Several interior doors were added to the otherwise open living
and dining area. He chose unpainted, and, ultimately, never
painted, hollow doors which did nothing to enhance the twelve
inch wide pine floorboards throughout the house made out of
original 1840 barn wood whose patina glowed richly in stark
contrast. Neither did the poorly assembled IKEA kitchen which
I was conscripted for days to help construct in the middle of
our living room. Today when I see photos of that gorgeous
home, my eye immediately goes to the kitchen cabinets with
poorly aligned doors and a small gap or two clearly visible. They

sat alongside bookcases, beds, computer desks and office furniture. Please don't take this as a knock on IKEA whose products are generally very well designed and useful. The gaps resulted from his over inflated sense of capabilities and my clear acknowledgement of mine.

Shortly after moving into our soon to be showcase on the hill, our own veritable Manor, we learned the Town had a Transfer Station. Any other town would have called it a *dump* but the very idea of anything as low class and ordinary as a dump existing in this picture perfect Connecticut setting sent a collective shudder town-wide through all the Armani shoulder pads right down to the Guccis and Manolo Blahniks. Best of all, there was no charge for day-to-day trash and garbage deposits of the sort that the local trash carting company regularly picked up for a fee. We decided to give the Transfer Station a try.

The drive from our home to the Transfer Station was beautiful and peaceful, especially in the early morning sunlight which was when we drove it. We looked forward to the time together at the start of the day. We brewed fresh coffee to take along with us in our identical and individually labeled insulated coffee mugs. We referred to these drives as our "Dump Dates." It was a happy time for us. We felt fortunate to be together and deeply content. Until we weren't. Or at least he wasn't.

In the middle of a snowstorm twelve years after we moved into The Manor Born, shoveling out, yet again, a friend, or the housekeeper, or a friend's friend, or the friend's housekeeper at the bottom of our long, steep, winding driveway, His Nibs leaned on the shovel, fat white flakes sticking to his stocking cap and his eyelashes. He turned to me and said, "I don't want to do this anymore." At the moment, I assumed he meant the whole deal.… the large property with all the upkeep, the shoveling out, the endless groundskeeping, the $22K a year real estate taxes.

"You are the one who physically takes care of 99% of all of this, so you get to make that decision," I responded. It was a tough decision to sell The Manor Born. We loved it and had many gatherings and events there. It was the physical and social centerpiece of our lives, our friends, our families. Family reunions. A post prom party and slumber party for 30 teenagers. Musical concerts, large and small dinner parties. The house was perfectly suited for entertaining, from intimate gourmet food and wine dinners on the barn roof covered deck overlooking the sloping three acres below, or large dinner parties with writers, consultants, our fascinating collection of friends and neighbors. We could host a dinner party for fifty on a day's notice. We had enough crystal, cutlery, plates, service platters, cooking pots, wine glasses, cordials, placemats and tablecloths on hand to make any occasion not only festive but large and festive.

Later we added on Baby Barn, a large barn structure connected to the main house by a short walkway sloping down the hill making three stories. The lower story was a beautiful apartment with a loft bed and a wall of windows and skylights opening up total views of the hillside. The second story was a three car garage, and over the garage encompassing the entire width of the structure was "The Room of Possibilities," complete with fireplace, skylights, an enormous table seating sixteen used by day if needed as a conference table, and in the evenings for grand dinner parties. A baby grand piano was also in the affectionately named Baby Barn where we hosted some of my early cabaret[3] shows, sneak previews for my New York club openings.

What I didn't know at the time was he'd already checked out.
Months later, in an uncharacteristic moment of reflection, he
admitted even he "didn't know it was over at the time," a non-
apologetic reflection in response to my pointing out the beauty-
ful Valentine's card and deeply intimate gift he'd given me only
a year before, seconds before both were flung in a tearful rage
into the trash can under the desk they were sitting on in a
prominent position.

In the fifteen months between selling The Manor Born and The
Great Shitstorm, now sometimes referred to by me as The
Great Plot Twist in a lame effort to reform and recalibrate my
life, we found The Idyllic Cottage Antique Barn, a carriage barn
built on an estate in the late 1880's, cozy and charming within a
fifteen minute bike ride to the Long Island Sound. It was,
however, unsuitable, and impractical, and much too small, but
he'd decided that's what he wanted during our transition
between Connecticut and the brass ring of Santa Barbara.

After downsizing and moving out of the enormous Manor, we
still had way too many clothes (especially him…), books (non-
fiction, literary fiction, cookbooks, sociology texts, my graduate
school texts, novels) office things (file cabinets, bookcases,
endless cups with endless pens and pencils, his beloved slant
desks he crafted everywhere) kitchen gadgets, and furniture, to
come close to fitting comfortably in the cottage. And, oh yes,
the clothes. Let's not forget the clothes.

He was a clothes horse. Our one long closet in the one tiny
bedroom was two-thirds consumed with his shirts, slacks, and
sports jackets. He loved to buy "top of the bottom" shirts at the
discount big box stores. They looked okay, mostly from a
distance, but up close I could see the thinness of the material
and the not quite matched up stripes and windowpane checks.

Many of our friends, fortunately for him, were academics themselves and did not notice.

Our Idyllic Cottage Antique Barn was close to a gritty, urban area with Interstate I-95, first place winner in the roadside visual pornography stakes, running through it. Traffic. Noise. The dump there was just that. A dump. Located next to the interstate, cars turned off onto the exit ramp, then onto the unabashedly tacky Main Street with its shabby pizza and tattoo parlors, nail salons, third-rate thrift stores and dry cleaners, making a right turn after a few hundred feet into the entrance to the dump. Once there we parked perpendicularly between white line spaces against a four-foot-high concrete barrier. Over the next few months I would open the tailgate and haul out each bag of garbage, trash, or debris one by one perfecting my pre-viously undiscovered wind up, working up into my signature overhead swing like a champion shot putter.

Years before, I lived with my second husband, Hyphen-Husband (who you will hear more about later) on Long Island in a converted boat barn with a park across the street. I watched Al Orter, four-time Olympic disc and shot put medal winner, practice for hours several times a week in the park, so my knowledge of good form is indisputable. Heaving the bags of trash and garbage over the barrier one by one, I watched each one sail through the air until it landed twenty feet below with a ridiculously satisfying splat on the covered concrete slab, nestled, finally, among dozens of other green bags, split open and revealing their stinking contents, along with broken office chairs, a child's pee-stained mattress, and other untethered garbage.

This was not the bucolic Fairfield County Transfer Station of The Manor Born. It was, frankly, disgusting. And it stank.

Badly. Layers of garbage and fouled diapers combined their odors in an impressive reek. After the first joint trip to the new dump the task of the bi-weekly dump runs fell to me, no longer a fitting use of time for His Nibs, and certainly no occasion for Dump Dates.

The Dump Meister, a wary, suspicious gentleman with gyroscopic eagle eyes, never stopped scanning the scene like a human lighthouse. He was charged with the Herculean task of making sure nothing outside the Dump Guidelines, posted every few feet so no one could possibly miss them, made its way to the concrete pit. Occasionally I had a bag that was extra heavy and I politely solicited his help with a lift of my eyebrow and a smile. I guess because no one ever approached The Dump Meister without a complaint about the Dump Rules, he was always happy to leave his small brown wooden observation hutch and help. We became Dump Buddies.

A year later, when The Great Plot Twist landed with a thud just like one of those garbage bags on the dark day of my mother's death in San Antonio, I knew I had to return as quickly as possible to the cramped Idyllic Cottage Antique Barn and sort through all our belongings once again. His Nibs returned to Santa Barbara to craft the details of his new life with his new partner.

I started with our closet. My clothes took up very little space, but when they were removed, I could see all the new space it opened for his cheap shirts and discount sports jackets. Over our years together he would occasionally enlist my help in "purging" his closets – getting rid of things he no longer wore or were, as he called it, "tired." Then, inspiration hit me.

He had *no* idea how many shirts he had, especially since many were near carbon copies of others; lots of blue checked shirts, blue striped shirts, boring identical out of style beige "work" shirts, many of which *were* tired looking, used up, with stained neck bands or worn cuffs. I would be doing him a service, I reasoned, thinning out the herd as we say in Texas, plus throwing out a few relatively newer ones which he would wonder for months where they went. The sport coats and blazers…really…he did not have especially good taste and several of these jackets were plainly outdated. Those ridiculous "shirt jacks" he was so taken with? The world would be a better place if no one ever had to see him or anyone in one of those again. I retrieved a couple of extra heavy-duty green garbage bags from the kitchen and went to town. A hanger here; a hanger there. I yanked off four dull beige ones with slightly worn cuffs; three or four small blue checked; a particularly (uncharacteristically) nice blue and white windowpane, a red striped.

After straightening out the hangars, I was surprised to see the thinning out was hardly noticeable. Why stop with shirts? I started in on the sports jackets. He was an odd size to just buy off the rack. Often the cuffs were just a *taaaaaad* short, the waists a *teensy* too loose even when buttoned. I selected six jackets, humming "Desperado" as I went about my task.

And then I saw it. The only good, exceptionally well-made piece of clothing in his entire wardrobe, bought on an impulse at a high-end non-discount men's store in Santa Barbara. I couldn't believe he'd given in to buy it, especially paying full price. It was a dark navy, high quality heavy wool Michael Kors pullover casual piece, with a stand-up collar lined in beautiful chocolate brown leather soft as butter. He looked fabulous in it and yes, I hate to admit it, when he wore it, he did look as if he were born to some Manor somewhere or other and, traffic-stopping fabulous.

It was perfect in weight, style, and class for chilly Santa Barbara evenings when going out to dinner sitting on the patio of Olio e Limon or the terrace of San Ysidro Ranch restaurant. Could I possibly? Dare I? Maybe everything, anything but that. I didn't hate him. I never did or have after all these years. Truly. But I did hurt – a lot – and at that moment, excruciatingly. I was furious at the pain he was inflicting without any sense of remorse or acknowledgment. But could I do *this*?

Damn straight I could. I yanked that beautiful puppy off its wooden hanger so hard the hanger went flying in the air and almost landed on my head. Would have served me right, and I didn't care. With a show of intentional cruelty, I wadded that sucker up, crammed it into the bag with the other stolen goods, and headed down to the car, jammed the bag in the back, gunned the motor, and drove as fast as I dared to the dump. I screeched to a halt in one of the primo slots. I jumped out and flung open the tailgate. I grabbed the dark green trash bag full of the incriminating evidence of the Great Closet Purge and swung it violently over my head once. I swung it twice. I swung it three times. Then, just as I was ready to give it a particularly energetic heave ho Al Orter would have been proud of, I stopped. My shoulders slumped. I dropped the bag at my feet.

The Dump Meister had seen me come screeching into the open slot followed by an agitated slamming of the brakes. He stood slack jawed watching the precision and energy of the heft and swing of the bag and knew something was up. With a concerned look he loped over.

"Are you OK, Miss? Do you need some help?" The first words spoken between us after more than a year. I shook my head no. I slowly walked back to the tailgate, swung it open over my head and shoved in the bag. Before closing the tailgate, I reached in the bag and randomly grabbed a single shirt. It turned out to be one of the particularly cheap blue and white windowpane ones. I shoved my hand in the bag again and grabbed a random sports jacket and closed the tailgate.

I looked at the Dump Meister with a look he intuitively understood to mean I wanted to toss these two individual pieces over the concrete barrier, a clear violation of Dump Rules, we both knew. He looked back at me with a tiny smile and shrug of his shoulders, turned around, and walked back to his hutch. With a careful windup, the shirt and the sports jacket went sailing over the barrier, caught for a few seconds on an updraft, then billowed down, coming to rest on the heap of garbage below. It took a few seconds for them to be covered in some green bean casserole detritus, topped with a headless Barbie doll. With a last look I got in the car and drove out of the dump, catching out of the corner of my eye the Dump Meister giving me a two-finger salute on the bill of his green ball cap. When I returned to the Idyllic Antique Cottage Barn I hung up the shirts and sports jackets, smoothing out the beautiful Michael Kors pullover as best I could, and rehung it.

When I think about that day, I still remember the surge of energy that electrified me as I ripped shirts and jackets off the hangers and stuffed them in the heavy green plastic bag with a carelessness not unlike today's poorly trained cashiers in his favorite men's big box stores. It was not about hurting him or raw revenge. Not really. I wanted to get him in one of the places where it hurt the most – his vanity about his looks and how he dressed. I wanted to reciprocate for how I was feeling, the way my sense of self-worth and pride felt decimated, wadded up like trash, intentionally, carelessly tossed away. I wanted to just drive him crazy, picturing with relish his puzzled look and then growing frustration, wondering where certain things could have disappeared to that he knew had just been there.

Later he would wonder where the graduated plastic bags of Allen wrenches were that he desperately needed to dismantle all the Ikea stuff on the day his moving van arrived, or the oddly missing Cialis tablets in his brand-new wheel of pills. Where did they go? Okay, maybe I do know something about those. I'm not perfect. I wanted him to wonder in frustration, just as I wondered now about when and where our intimacy, companionship, sense of fun, and intellectual partnership had disappeared to.

I didn't grow up with expectations about what is required of folks who are To the Manor Born. I'm not sure I knew what a Manor was until much later, much less the Rules for belonging. But I did grow up with many years of Sunday School and Vacation Bible School and "doing the right thing." Although I had abandoned that spiritual framework many years before, I guess a lot of it sank in deeper than I knew. Somewhere that day I decided that turning the other cheek was a better way to live with myself than festering with bitterness, sowing the seeds for a life of victimhood, wasting my time and libido creating revenge scenarios. I'm not really a bunny boiler.

That day I felt like the Manor was mine. I recalled a long-forgotten Bible verse I'd learned as a child, one that really didn't make much sense to me, other than, as a child, I misconstrued the actual meaning. "In my Father's House are many mansions. If it were not so, I would have told you." Was a mansion like a Manor, I wondered? If so, then I'd arrived in mine. The Manor felt like I had always imagined such a place should look and feel. Kind of like Ireland. Free. Open. Green. Except even better. My conscience was clear. Well. Clear enough for now.

Maybe that's why I have difficulty with the idea of forgiveness. It's not a one and done. Acceptance and moving on need to find their own pace. My job is to recognize the little steps for what they are, tiny and erratic, important, not to be discounted even if it is just a shirt or two instead of a whole closet.

Yes. That was progress.

3 – When Life Throws You A Curve, Hit The Road

Well, look. Everything that we got to lose is gone anyway.

~ Thelma Dickinson, *Thelma and Louise*

To be honest, I was inclined to work out my life with a kick-off and kick-ass road trip anyway.

I started road trips early in life, with long family drives back and forth between Virginia and the District of Columbia area to San Antonio, home of Fort Sam Houston, the headquarters of the Medical Service Corp, the branch of the Army in which Daddy served. In those days my older brother Mike and I were tossed in the back of the family station wagon on a blanket or quilt, armed with a supply of comic books: Archie and Veronica and Beetle Bailey. This was long before the days of *Mad Magazine* which Mike became addicted to when he got older, the beginning of my knowledge that boys and girls, and later, men and women, generally had totally different tastes in those things.

I remember those trips as long stretches of boredom, my brother and I desperate to make the time pass. Bickering and blaming got old early. We couldn't even argue about who was claiming the hump in the middle of the floor, or who was taking up too much room, because we owned the entire cargo area of the station wagon. All our suitcases were placed with geometric precision on the roof of the car, tied down with fifty feet of rope. My brother and I grasped desperately, and often creatively, at random straws to eliminate boredom. We counted four footed creatures we saw out of our side of the car, praying

we would not see a white horse or cemetery requiring us to start
all over again. Those were the rules of the road and we felt
oddly honor bound to acknowledge them. That was my older
brother even then, driven by honor and fairness, and I respected that, even though I was tempted often to pretend not to
notice the white horse in the field we'd just passed on my side
of the road. We logged state license plates. We read comic
books on our stomachs on top of the quilts laid out in the bed
of the station wagon. No seat belts for any of us. We loved
reading the Burma Shave signs printed on rough slabs of wood
and later more sophisticated red and white printed billboards,
showing up unexpectedly around a curve in the middle of
nowhere.

As an adult, curious about how they came about and the story
behind them (there had to be a story behind the stories), I did
some research. In the beginning in the 1920's, Alan Odell was
selling Burma Shave cream, a product produced by his father in
Minnesota. There were usually a set of four or five signs posted
about one hundred feet apart and early ones didn't even rhyme.
They were originally spaced to be best read going thirty-five
miles an hour, probably not unusual on all the back two-lane
roads across the south and mid-west plains that we traveled
over. In all those years, on all those trips, I don't remember ever
seeing a duplicate.

<table>
<tr><td>

Is he lonesome
Or just blind
The guy who drives
So close behind?

</td><td>

My job is keeping
Faces clean
And nobody knows
The stubble I've seen.

</td></tr>
</table>

… and on and on for over one hundred "verses" over many
years.

The worst times were the hours stuck in some dusty southern town at some old gas station that may or may not have a big metal cooler on legs where I could plunge my arm into the freezing water up to my elbow and retrieve a Nehi orange or grape soda. The detours in these towns were usually because a fan belt had broken or the engine had overheated, or a tire with a slow leak had finally gone flat, or some such common occurrence in those days. It was a common site seeing cars on the side of the road with their hoods propped up on the single metal hood lift. No one had phones of course, so I guess Daddy must have trudged down the road until he found a phone booth somewhere or got a lift with a stranger to the closest gas station for a tow truck. It was an inevitable part of every trip, but it was okay. We just reread our comics again, or walked around town, which didn't take long. One time my brother and I found a package of Fig Newtons in the car Mom had managed to keep hidden, so we ate them all while waiting for rescue, much to our gastro regret later. To this day I don't like Fig Newtons much, but that day, shaking out the bag for the last crumbs to fight over, I thought they were pretty fine.

On the good days of those early family road trips, we might end up at Myrtle Beach at the small amusement park riding the carousel and eating an ice cream cone, a rare treat. Or, (oh heaven!) end up in a motel with a swimming pool, eagerly anticipating that first running jump regardless of how greenish the water might be with the bobbing of a single high top tennis shoe floating in it. Many days we drove into the night because we needed to make "good time."

We traveled through the deep south because that was just the way we knew to go. It was familiar to my parents, I guess. A few mental remnants still come clearly to mind about some of those trips. I remember the steep metal bridge across the

Mississippi taking us into Vicksburg, which even then to my young eyes seemed dirty and crowded. I remember the water fountains for Coloreds and Whites on the town greens or next to the gas stations in the small southern towns we drove through. We often spent mind-numbing, hot, dusty hours while we waited for a fan belt to be replaced, or the oil leak to be finally identified. Once I asked my mother about the signs on the water fountains. She said different folks had to use different things, that's all.

I had grown up hearing my mother's mother talk about Nigras and coming from thirteen generations of tobacco farmers from the same little town, Republican Grove, in southern Virginia, forty-four miles from Appomattox, it was just the way things were. I guess they were the same way in Richmond, Virginia where Daddy grew up. It didn't occur to me to question it. Growing up in a military family and attending my first element-ary school on post, I'd always grown up with kids and families who were Black, Asian, Hispanic, so while it wasn't a big deal to hear it was just the way it was, it didn't make sense on some level that would later blossom into genuine questioning as I got older.

We always took "the southern route" back and forth between Washington, D.C. and San Antonio because that's what was familiar, the geography of the small towns we drove through in Virginia, Mississippi, and Alabama, as well as the culture of the south, the segregation, regional accents, and just fitting in. There were no interstates at the time, at least in the south, so we didn't have the option of by-passing these small towns. There was only one way, and that was through. I realized later in life what a good metaphor that is for a lot of life's change and difficulties. "You can adjust, or you can adjust," as was often said in my family.

The thing I dreaded most on these family road trips through the south was being behind the huge trailer trucks of massive logs coming out of the deep piney woods on their way to somewhere else. The two-lane roads were narrow and not necessarily straight in most places as we wound our way through the endless southern forests. The hilly sections made it hard to see around the enormous trailers of logs. After trailing behind one of these trucks for an eternity, and seeing my father's growing impatience, I could sense what was coming. My stomach knotted with that sick foreshadowing of needing to throw up. I was terrified to look and more terrified to not look. I couldn't *not* look. Daddy looked back and around as much as he could, time after time, and finally, he'd pull out into the other lane and floor the car, and for what seemed like forever we'd be flying along into blindness, parallel with that massive trailer loaded with logs. Would the logs topple down on us? Would we be able to outrun it, and if we did would there be nothing coming on the other side? Questions that made my throat freeze, thankfully, since screaming at the top of my lungs would not, I'm very sure, have improved the situation. There was a fragrant blast of pine as our Ford station wagon (always a Ford) labored in parallel with the monster of our potential undoing, sometimes along with the ear shattering screech of gear as if it were trying to maintain or better its speed. Why was I the only one who seemed terrified about the inevitable? If my mother and brothers were equally terrified, they were able to pull the "let's not show any emotion" face, a Morgan family specialty, quietly blinking, or, in my older brother's case, reading his comics.

Today on an eight-lane interstate I can see one of those monster zillion-foot long logging trucks and I'm struck with the same terror…will the chains holding all those logs break free jamming them through the windshield of my car? Will they carrom out of their lane, jack-knifing across the entire eight lanes creating a twenty car pileup, or tumble cab over axle out of control down the side of the mountain? Why did those very long, almost vertical "runaway truck lanes" on the side of the road offer no reassurance? There are some childhood terrors that do not resolve with time, I am here to testify. Some days I feel I have magically exchanged the child in the back seat on a blind pass of the logging truck with the woman who's launched into one blind relationship after another, holding my breath and holding on for dear life, relieved more than I should be to survive one more terrifying stretch of life, even if just for a while, which it usually is.

What is it about road trips? Why did the idea leap to mind so quickly as a way to begin the more important journey to survival, at the minimum, and restoration, at best? What difference would it make, really? Does the very idea just tap into our ancient DNA because we were all wanderers and gatherers for hundreds of thousands of years, moving with the seasons to the pastures of higher and lower ground, not unlike today's Snowbirds, evading threats from invaders and intruders? Even with GPS and cell phones today there is always the possibility of unplanned experiences, new acquaintances, serendipity and, in my case, the almost impossible feat of getting lost anyway. Siri and I have never become close friends. A road trip required the clear and intentional uncoupling from day-to-day routines and places where I was already floundering.

In my world there is always an accompanying musical track that colors and transforms my life forever on and to this day with vivid memories.

During the summer of 1963 I was traveling with my family across the deep South again from Washington, D.C. to San Antonio – Mother, Daddy, me, two brothers, my grandmother, and my parakeet, Perry, holding on for dear life in his miniscule traveling cage on the rear window shelf of the burgundy Ford Fairlane sedan. Feathers and birdseed flew, all of us grimacing as we leaned into what Daddy called our 460 Air Conditioner – four windows down going 60 miles an hour – (cue his self-congratulatory laughter) occasionally picking seed out of our teeth, and straining to listen to "Surfing USA," or "It's My Party," or the insipid "Sukiyaki," or, (sweet Jesus) bluegrass and Bill Monroe if Mother and Daddy had control of the radio dial. The Appalachian mountain music my parents had grown up with sounded like chickens squawking to my brothers and me. I had my thirty minutes of control time of the dial, as everyone in the family did, and I prayed desperately my thirty minutes did not coincide with a section of the back woods road that could not get a signal. There were no allowances or compensation for that lost time in the family dial rotation power algorithm. As Daddy said, "Them's the breaks, Honey. Life's not always fair." No indeed, Daddy. No indeed it isn't.

Years later, after my second year of college at Texas Tech, the road trip soundtrack memory trigger was Bob Dylan crooning "Lay Lady Lay" driving across the endless miles of West Texas, hot and dusty and full of August 1969. I was flying eighty-five miles an hour over empty West Texas roads with no posted speed limit in my Totally Unsuitable Bad Boy Boyfriend's red 1962 Chevy convertible, cruising through prairies and deserts on our way to Glorieta Baptist Assembly fifteen miles outside of Santa Fe. Yes. Glorieta. A sprawling 2400-acre Southern Baptist summer encampment campus site with dorms and cabins and small hotel-like accommodations for over 2000 guests each week over the ten-week summer season, set like a beautiful diamond jewel in the Sangre de Cristo mountains. All the jobs on campus – dorm maids, cafeteria cooks and servers, stable hands, landscapers and garden tenders, ice cream shop clerks – were filled by college-age staff from Baptist churches across the country – hundreds of them, of which I was one for six weeks for two summers. Glorieta. It was a beautiful ranch with mountains and a manmade lake and nice accommodations. There was lots to do and interesting (for good Christian families) "themes" for each of the weeks, such as Sunday School Week, Music Week, and Missions Week. Yes, they actually spent a week talking about Sunday School. It was especially paradise for a college age young man or young woman working there, toiling for the glory of Jesus, of course. Whether wandering together in the wild mountain woods, stopping every so often for…well…you know…or holding hands in the Prayer Garden in the morning devotionals with Brother Earl, the memory of the juxtaposition of those two things, perpetually smoldering potential sex and ever-present Jesus, still torques my brain. Totally Unsuitable Bad Boy Boyfriend and I were headed there one summer for College Week, the last week of the season, when those 2000 guests were also college students. Holy Moly.

My Totally Unsuitable Bad Boy Boyfriend had zero life prospects. He had dropped out of college to "find himself." He was a legitimate, integrity filled (if not sanctimoniously bursting at the seams) conscientious objector[4] at the height of the Vietnam War, spending all his time working on the endless intimidating documentation required of someone seeking that classification. Years later he told me it was harder, more complicated, and more emotionally and physically intensive than writing his PhD dissertation. His father, who he was very close to, was on the draft board of the small central Texas town where he grew up, making the whole episode painful for everyone. He was the first person in the history of the town to apply as a conscientious objector, and had to appear in front of the board, looking directly at his father, who, he said, was supportive all along the way, even though he did not understand it.

I certainly didn't. I was The Colonel's Daughter, used to a life where the mantra "rank has its privilege" was ingrained from an early age, the rules for life and values were always crystal clear, serving in the military for young men being one. It was a combination that provided endless conflict and heat of course, and, correspondingly, unbridled sexual passion. We fought. We cried. He pleaded. It was all drama all the time, something I must have craved after all the years of military discipline, rule following, coloring within all the lines. Despite the impossibilities of our relationship that summer I was compellingly, magnetically attracted to him for many reasons, all of them sexual, one being the unencumbered front bench seat in his red Chevy convertible. The heat from that trip is still accessible to me, memories and physical responses I can summon up at will over fifty years later, usually, at inconvenient moments.

After the shock of The Great Shitstorm and the day of Double-Barreled Heartbreak, I was inspired to begin a road trip by my vast, rich, classical, literary, and cinematic inner life. I was an Army Brat, used to picking up at least every few years and starting over, reinventing myself in a new place with new friends, a new story. Now I was outright desperate to explore friends and family and venues over an extended time. The mythic attractions of road trips like Odysseus' – the leave taking, the adventure making, the danger seeking, and ultimately the homecoming – had a firm grip on my teenage imagination, and they still do. I had no equivalent of Helen, or in my case, His Nibs, waiting for me at the end, clearly. And let's not forget the Children of Israel, although forty years wandering inhospitable territory, second in my book only to West Texas, did not particularly appeal to me, or to them either, probably, but who am I to quibble with the Bible?

Years later, after many years of Sunday School stories, especially those of the Apostle Paul and his, what seemed to me through my child's perspective, wildly dramatic, voyages, I fell in love with Jack Kerouac and *On the Road* and yearned for a road trip – without the drugs and jazz and desire to burn, burn, burn like the mad ones of course, rather my own Texas sweetheart Hallmark movie version of one, but a road trip, nonetheless. John Steinbeck's *Travels with Charlie* created the longing for a fine dog to travel with which I never quite managed because I never had a dog that didn't instantly throw up when I got him in the car. I always envied friends whose dogs went everywhere with them. I fell in love with Clark Gable and Claudette Colbert for the first, if not the fiftieth time, watching the racy, smart, stylish film classic *It Happened One Night.* When Clark Gable hung that blanket between the twin beds in the motor court tourist cabin, with clothespins and great determination, I swooned.

Audrey Hepburn and Albert Finney made me fall in love with Provence, creating an intense yearning for a road trip through southern France that was fulfilled thirty years later with His Nibs. The gorgeously filmed *Two for the Road* irritated me at the time because this beautiful, sexy couple wasted so much time fighting and arguing, although today I see how honestly it portrayed a long-term relationship, something I had no experience with at that time and barely can say I have today. There were silent cast members, other stars of the film, a string of fantastically beautiful cars including a Mercedes 230L Roadster and an MG that I loved even when, or perhaps because, it burst into flames. That film and those cars have gone on to make me feel a lesser being on any trip I've ever been on or in every car I've ever owned. The film had a Henry Mancini and Leslie Bricusse award winning song by the same name which haunted me so long and so deeply I could finally only excise its grip on my psyche and soul by including it in one of my New York City cabaret shows. The show was titled "Song for the Open Road," and the movie song was "Two for The Road," which won an Oscar (the song, not me). I eventually did have the car of my dreams inspired by that movie, a 1996 Jaguar XJ6 named Ruby. Beautiful. Flawless. Low to the road with a quiet purr and pristine buff colored leather interior. Her license plate read "RubyQ," named for the color of Santa Barbara Qupe Syrah, the favorite "girls' drinking wine" during happier, freer times years before. It was a sad day when I had to sell that beauty a few years later to pay off some of the credit card debt His Nibs had run up and was not able to pay. She (Ruby) would have been heaven on a Road Trip. Neither of us ever forgave him.

Most road trip/getaway fantasy films were men's territory. The films were mainly stupid ones in my opinion, with the occasional classic: *Easy Rider; Midnight Cowboy; The Motorcycle Diaries*, but the film *Thelma and Louise* electrified me and my women friends. I was unprepared for what I experienced as the truth of it. It simultaneously enraged men with its themes of rebel housewife runaway adventures on a road trip, wanton sex, outright floozy behavior, unbridled drinking, complete with a genuine Boy Toy and a Brad Pitt one at that. Perhaps it just pulled all the cultural triggers of the day. The fact that it didn't appear to end well or genteelly, even though terribly dramatic, only made the adventure more thrilling, and a pointed cautionary tale to women about coloring outside the lines. Or, as my mother once told me when I did not change my name when I got married, "When you flaunt convention, honey, you've got to expect some difficulties." Or maybe it was because Thelma said, "Sometimes all you need is a great friend and a tank of gas." There's not a woman alive who's old enough to drive who doesn't resonate like a tuning fork to the truth of that statement. Decades later, the film's ending stirs passionate debate among just about all the women I know as to whether it was a good ending or bad ending or just inevitable, and a metaphor for women's lives in general. God, I love those conversations.

I believed at the time a road trip, whether by car or air, was just what I needed to sort through the enormous changes I'd been handed. I had no idea for how long or where. I trusted that would all emerge. I needed to understand the sudden U-turn in my life that had tackled me completely unawares, and to figure out how I got to this place in my life at this age. Did I really have terrible taste in men, as one of my High School Girl Gang had declared? Or maybe I wanted and expected too much, as my mother insisted. Regardless of the cause, I needed to figure out some things, just the way Thelma and Louise and Jack Kerouac had. But look how it turned out for them.

Distance to Empty

Music and Lyrics by Chick Morgan ©2014

Long stretch of lonesome flying by
I'm running away from your goodbye.
Miles behind me, more to go
Dashboard says empty is closer than I know.
Too many miles behind me to go back from where I came
Scenery keeps changing, pain feels the same.
Distance to empty is staring at me.
If I can't learn to let go it's empty I'm gonna be.

Drinking my way down from you leaving me
Wine's here to help drown away your memory.
One drink I tell myself, well, maybe one more
Distance to empty - the bottle's keeping score.
Too many drinks behind me to go back from where I came
Vintages keep changing, pain feels the same
Distance to empty is staring at me
And if I can't find a way to stop it's empty, I'm gonna be.

Trying to forget you or at least let you go
Mind says move on. Heart says go slow.
Broken dreams behind me but maybe I can find
A way to fill this emptiness and leave heartbreak behind
Distance to empty is staring at me
If I can't learn to let you go it's empty, I'll always be.

4 – One For The Road

Calling a taxi in Texas is like calling a rabbi in Iraq.

~ Fran Liebowitz

The car is a traveling hermitage.

~Father James Finlay

In my life I have crashed on the moon, gotten lost in the desert, been capsized at sea, and become lost in the woods on a remote mountainside. Sort of.

There was a decade or so when a certain type of "group learning experience" was popular. They all ran along the themes of "Crashed on the Moon," "Lost in the Desert," "Crashed in the Desert," "Crashed in the Woods," "Capsized at Sea." Each executive team of eight to twelve members imagined a catastrophe that upended business. To say these were gender skewed in the extreme seems obvious now, but not so much then. There was no "Lost in the Mall with Four Screaming Kids," or "Dumped by Your Husband at Sixty-Four" for instance.

Let's take "Crashed in the Woods." The description of the event came with a list of fifteen or twenty miscellaneous items that managed to survive the crash – a book of matches, a bottle of gin, a rope, an ax, an old Playboy Magazine, for example. Only ten or twelve of whatever items were found could be salvaged, or at least be useful.

The first task for the team was to decide: Do we stay put so a rescue party can find us, or do we go and seek help and hope to find rescue? There was always controversy and good arguments on either side. It was ultimately the most important decision on which all other decisions depended. Would the team wander aimlessly, or figure out how to go about their wandering? Should they split up? Should they stay put and wait for rescue?

"If we set out, how do we know where we are or where we are going?"

"What if we get lost?"

"What if we get separated?"

"How can we carry all the supplies?"

"Should one or two people stay behind or should we all stay behind?"

"How will 'they' find us if we leave this place?"

Regardless of whether the team had taken the time to figure out the "stay or go" question, they had to prioritize the list of items in terms of importance. They couldn't keep them all. Most teams that I worked with over a couple of decades blew past the "should we stay or should we go" conversation and got straight to figuring out who would go where and how far, fighting over whether to prioritize, among other things, matches, gin, a deck of cards, and lengths of rope.

Somewhere in the emotional disarray of those early days of The Great Shitstorm when my emotions ran rampant between fear and anger, I felt a similar confusion. I couldn't go to Santa

Barbara yet – or ever. I couldn't stay in Connecticut. All my instincts told me I had to keep moving. But where? How? I had no on-going income for the moment and assets, such as they were, were going to be tied up for some time to come. How was I going to figure this out?

I was driving through Westport, Connecticut, frantically running errands after my initial return from the Santa Barbara debacle and my mother's proper and loving burial in San Antonio, trying to figure out what and how to pack and get out of the Idyllic Antique Cottage Barn before His Nibs got back from his most recent tryst in Santa Barbara. I thought about getting a storage unit, which is not as easy as it sounds. With Baby Boomers downsizing and couples of all ages splitting up and kids coming home from college with their own stuff and needing to move in with mom and dad, every storage unit company had a waiting list.

How could I decide what to take when I had no idea where I was heading or how I'd be living? Do I haul it (whatever small collection of stuff by that time made up the "it") across the country to Santa Barbara when I didn't even know if I'd be living there? Do I sell it all and say what the hell and start from scratch – *again?* Do I find another storage unit in Connecticut making me a bi-coastal storage stuff hoarder, a featured episode on Storage Wars? Do I find another place here in Westport for the time being and hopefully figure all this out? But how could I figure out all this heartbreak and upheaval unless I got out of this place? I've always been resilient. I had to be, to be an Army brat. I've always had that so-called Texas Grit. Should I stay or should I go?

I drove down Kings Highway in Westport, and over the small bridge crossing the Saugatuck River where even the picturesque mallards that called the small, rough stream home were huddling and shivering on that bleak early March afternoon. The end of winter rain pounded cold spikes drowning my windshield. I barely noticed. My phone rang in my car. Oh, God. I can't talk to anyone right now. I can barely even drive. My sobs were obliterating what little sight there was through the windshield. It was my sister-in-law calling from Texas. I hit Accept. This is what unconditional love sounds like:

"Mike (my brother) and I have been talking, trying to figure out what we can do to help you right now, and here's what we want you to do. Go to a bank, different from your regular bank. Open a new account. We will transfer money immediately. We never want to know what you do with it or have any accounting of it or speak of it again. Just do what you need to be able to do right now." It was the first of several times over the next couple years I would ask myself, "Who gets family like this?" Well, I guess I do.

I did, and they did. Suddenly I began to imagine how to make a nourishing space to travel and find out what was next. I needed to disengage from the chaos and heartbreak. I had never shared my thoughts with anyone about traveling for a few months in different locations not tied so closely to our life, creating space to think, mourn, and separate.

I was newly unpartnered. My Children of Affection (as my stepdaughters and I referred to each other) were grown, miraculously, and improbably fledged. I didn't have pets to worry about. Our (his really) ancient infirmed three-legged cat with a heart problem had conveniently hobbled across The Rainbow Bridge a few weeks before we went to Santa Barbara. It seemed to be the comically perfect metaphor for the entire

Shitshow I was going through: a relationship on its last four, well, three, legs, about to give up the ghost.

Like every other hapless crashee in all the Crashed on the Moon/Woods/Desert/Sea exercises, I was doing precisely what all the content creator experts argued authoritatively was *not* the thing to do under any circumstances anywhere or anytime. To a man, and it was always a man, they lectured that everyone should stay put at the crash scene. I decided *not* to stay put and wait for rescue to find me. I would light my candles with the match, I would drink the gin straight, I would find someone to play poker with, and I would take the damn rope to lasso a star.

Once I decided to "go," how would I decide where or when or for how long?[5]

Years earlier on a trip to Ireland with His Nibs I learned about the Peregrinatio, someone who left his homeland in self-imposed exile and wandered, not necessarily for the love of God, but with a purpose, nonetheless. That sounded about right, but which homeland, I had to ask myself now? I'd already gladly abandoned Texas, and now I was abandoning the dreams of both my east coast and west coast homes. It could be an inner journey with no set destination. Yes, it sounded right again.

I knew I wasn't the classic Pilgrim, journeying for a religious or spiritual destination or outcome, although I hoped for some new spiritual awareness and guidance.

For me, the so-called idyllic homeland was an ordinary happy relationship, but to me, that felt like a "fantastic journey." At sixty-four, that ordinary happy relationship was receding further away in danger of disappearing entirely beneath the horizon. I never could quite believe Julia Roberts' character in the film *Notting Hill,* when she declares to Hugh Grant's character at the romantic climax, "Some people do spend their whole lives together." Well, you couldn't prove that by me.

I didn't have a plan. I didn't know if I'd be on the road for two weeks or two years. I decided it would take as long as it took. I didn't know where I'd be going or who would be open to seeing me or if I wanted to see anyone at all. The daily ricochet of being unmoored, liberated, unpartnered, unfettered, and frequently, very afraid, was exhausting. Mostly, I felt too old to do this again. This time was different than when I was rebuilding at twenty-six, and again at forty-eight. This was hard and terrifying. It didn't help that reasonably happily married women in seemingly good relationships with men I liked, men I considered the good guys, friends of long standing, looked at me with unnerving candor and said things that were some version of "I envy you."

Was Nora Ephron right when she wrote: "The desire to get married, which, I regret to say, I believe is basic and primal in women, is followed almost immediately by an equally basic and primal urge which is to be single."

Looking back, I wish there were other things I'd thought to do, like walk the Via di Santiago di Compostela which I would learn about years later. Or rent that idyllic stone cottage on the sea in Ireland that I landed upon with a girlfriend six years later. I didn't dream big enough. Lesson learned. For now, each morning was a new decision and a new opportunity. All I could handle was each day as it came and often not even that. I knew no matter what I did I would be back and forth to Texas to stay with my brother and sister-in-law in Wimberley to have access to Daddy in San Antonio about an hour away. It was more than past time to take some of the day-to-day heavy lifting of caretaking my brother and sister-in-law had lovingly, gracefully, and always uncomplainingly shouldered. Again, I asked myself, "Who has a family like that?" It turns out I do.

A few things were becoming clear. I needed *not* to be in Connecticut long term. I needed to move out of my home with the man I always thought I would be together with until we both toddled over from old age. Weren't we the couple who'd created a multi-day retreat experience for other couples not quite as enlightened as we to examine how to grow old together in a changing relationship? We were. I needed quiet. I needed healing space. I was exhausted from not sleeping and on edge from the loud and jangly non-stop script of failure running an endless loop in my head.

I needed to be in Wimberley to have concentrated time to be with Daddy. In addition to losing my mother, he lost his wife of seventy-four years, his soulmate, his partner. I needed to find a rhythm of time with him. With his cognitive decline, although he recognized me every time I walked in the door and was surprised and expressed pleasure at my arrival, he did not remember that I was there the hour before, or day before, or the day before that. That's okay. I knew. I got the bonus of seeing love and surprise on his face every time I walked in, even if it were five times a day. What greater gift could I give him? Creating a rhythm was as much for my brother and sister-in-law to know what to expect and when some caretaking relief was available as it was for Daddy or me. It would have to be in and out, casual, intermittent. I still found the idea of Texas for the long term intolerable.

It was clear I needed to be in Wimberley to focus on Mom, her life, her passing. The week she died was a blur with so many overlapping emotions of her death so quickly, and my husband ending the marriage on the same day. I have not been able to differentiate whether it was grief for my dying mother or my dying relationship or if it even mattered. I was not attempting to make a distinction. I lumped it all together into one big bucket of overwhelming grief and went with it. I knew when the tangled knot of emotional threads began to untangle, I may need to separate the two and honor each and work with each. Or maybe it was a distinction without a difference, as the saying goes.

A few weeks later when staying again with my brother and sister-in-law in Wimberley, I woke just past dawn in my comfortable bed. I lay there, aware of comforters, the books lining the shelves in the room around me, the birds beginning to stir and sing. Just peace. I padded out into the quiet kitchen and smelled the coffee that was already dripping down and on its way to me. A special coffee cup was set out for me, a pottery cup with hand painted Texas bluebonnets. It was warming, rim side down, on top of the coffee pot. Genius.

It was a foggy morning as I sat on the beautiful, covered porch. I began to wander the natural gardens that my sister-in-law had created and nurtured. The wisteria was in full bloom, reminding me of the morning of The Call.

I had been reading *To Pause at the Threshold: Reflection on Living on the Border* by Esther de Waal, a gift given to me by my beautiful Connecticut Dancing Diva friend, Inese. It is about thresholds and intentionally acknowledging and honoring them and learning from being *in* them, not just passing through on the way to somewhere else. The early pages reminded me of the importance of ritual, something I wanted to intentionally create every day.

My road trip had begun in earnest with these initial visits with Daddy in Wimberley. At first the travel was mostly back and forth between my new home base at my friends' beautiful home in Easton, Connecticut. Lush lawns and, a little later in the spring, beautiful flowers and shrubs, would greet my view every morning. Leaving the elegant beauty of the quiet verdant Connecticut countryside and coming back to Wimberley off and on helped create a demarcation of my times in such different places for different reasons. Staying in the quiet beauty of Wimberley and the Hill Country was a welcome relief from the drive to San Antonio and Daddy's health care facility down Interstate 35, frantic with eighteen wheelers whizzing by at speeds past the limit. It was also clotted and chaotic with huge pickup trucks crisscrossing madly and swerving between lanes, followed by massive gravel carriers spewing rocks and dust and gravel all along their route – twice onto my windshield producing dangerous cracks resulting in new windshields. The noise and chaos instilled a paralyzing fear of the drive to San Antonio each time I turned onto the highway. My early rhythm alternated between Connecticut to pick up mail, swap out clothes, attend to some professional work I was engaged with, touch base with my Connecticut friends like the Divas and Jack and others, then back to Wimberley so I could spend a few days if not a week with Daddy, back to Wimberley and back to Connecticut.

One Connecticut visit brought a long overdue gathering of The Divas, the group of talented, brilliant, extraordinary women friends of mine in Connecticut who come together ultimately to witness each other's lives and celebrate all things feminine – spirituality, professional networking, sageing circles, fashion,

jewelry, shoes, and good wine, among others. This gathering
was especially sweet as it was the first gathering I'd been to
since before the end of the previous year and when the Great
Shitstorm began in this one. I'd been dealing with Mom's death,
and the back and forth between Wimberley, San Antonio, and
Connecticut, but mostly my spirit didn't feel up to gatherings of
any kind, intense or otherwise. The prospect had felt too
overwhelming for the last few months, but that weekend it felt
right and good and it was. I was ready. One of the rituals we
often engage in when we gather is the reading of cards. We've
drawn from many decks over the years – feminine, spirit and
animal worlds, tarots of many sorts – but this deck of cards,
Angel Cards, was new to me.

It had been several months since my initial shock of those early
days. I'd begun to emerge from the initial pain, confusion, and
hurt, like someone emerging from an Oklahoma storm cellar
after a tornado, carefully, cautiously lifting the cellar door and
peering around at the scattered wreckage everywhere. Over
there, crushed under the oak tree was my sense of worth. There,
peeking out from under the roof of what used to be a garage
was my self-respect. Tossed on top of a pile of debris of clothes
and canned goods was my future. And just over there, barely
visible under the jagged back yard fence gate but still beating
weakly, was my very banged up and bruised heart.

Emerging on wobbly legs from the cellar, I climbed out, brush-
ing off the dust and grime of months of hunkering down in the
unimaginably small space of what had become my life. I'd begun
to think about my next stage, my next home, my kitchen with
my favorite pots and pans and Italian dinnerware and hand
thrown pottery mugs, my fireplace with maybe some antique
andirons or a rustic fire screen and hearth, dinner parties again,
which I'd always loved, and weekend guests. I had no idea

where, but I knew it was out there. When it came time to draw a card with the Divas, I drew VISION. The text read: "Look at the world with your soul sight. Use your imagination, inner sense, and peripheral promptings to see the bigger picture and shape the future you desire." Perfect.

Much of what I was learning on the trip with Mother Road, even at the beginning, was helping me "look at the world with soul sight" in what would turn out to be beautiful locations in which I found myself week after week, each offering the perfect visual anchoring point for what I needed at that moment. The Celtic mystic philosopher and poet, John O'Donohue, wrote, "Beauty is the illumination of the soul." My soul was being illuminated with each beautiful location in which I spent time. The Shaman Hernan reflected that "beauty is healing" and indeed it was for me. The beauty of landscapes, hillscapes, and seascapes would each speak its beauty to me in its unique way and at precisely the right time. With the hindsight of many miles on the ground and in the air, perspective was beginning to emerge.

I realized over the coming months each space I was privileged to visit offered me a place of beauty from which to meditate, sit, read, and drink my morning coffee out of a special mug. In my Easton, Connecticut home, that space had been a small jewel of a deck right off my bedroom, the Juliet Balcony my friends call it. It was on that deck, with the first cup of steaming coffee, when the precious early light of dawn seeped into the bedroom, I enjoyed the coziness of the balcony and the view over lovely Bradford pear trees in their full white dress, artisanal red and white heritage roses, pink azaleas, amethyst rhododendrons, and lush lawn. It was on that deck I experienced the continuity of place off and on over months as I watched the terrible winter of sadness evolve into the spring of renewal and rebirth. It didn't strike me until many months later that my favorite mug I chose each early morning in their kitchen was from The Mercy Center, an organization my friend was committed to, devoting many hours tutoring math to adult women preparing for their GED. My time there, and in their friendship and care, was a Mercy Center of its own.

During some of the earliest days of the Great Plot Twist I was still reeling from being torqued between Santa Barbara where His Nibs and I had been living for a few months, San Antonio with my mother's death and my father's need, Wimberley where I was offered safe harbor and a good bed during my visits to Daddy, and the east coast which became my Home Base for the road trip months. I was blessed with beautiful views.

Still trying to figure out which way was up or out in Santa Barbara, I stayed there for a while with long term friends in their mountaintop home with a long view that looked across a stone wall from their patio over an exquisite native plants garden, across the mountain and down to the ocean. Standing there early in the morning on that patio, the chill still in the air requiring a wrap or jacket or bathrobe, coffee cup in hand, I breathed in the scents of eucalyptus, bougainvillea, and the sea, looking across into infinity, meditating, reading. Often I just sat and tried to be.

For as long as I could remember, good friends had repeatedly invited us to spend time in their stunning art filled ocean front condo on the Outerbanks of North Carolina, and of course we repeatedly turned them down in the name of being too busy, or something else. But now when I was offered, I said of course, and thank you. I was uncertain if I could sustain complete solitude. I had no one in my life to call and no one who was checking in with me. I had, at the time of the invitation, been completely alone for most of the three months since my world changed in one day. I didn't know if I was ready, but the gift of time in the oceanfront condo gave me the answer.

It was still quite chilly, late April on the Atlantic ocean. I awakened at 5:00 each morning with no prompting and walked out to the dark living room that faced the soon-to-be rising sun, sat in a comfortable chair, my cup of coffee prepared the evening before with a timer, in a pottery mug with a lively seaside motif, sometimes a starfish, sometimes a saucy crab, and sat there watching the world quickly turn from barely rose to blazing sun – all right before my eyes. As the day warmed in the early afternoon I set out with my tunes and headphones, still bundled against the slightly chilly breezy day, and walked along the beach in utter solitude. Not a single soul to be seen. Morning after morning I played the album composed by my long-time New York cabaret musical director, Rick Jensen, with one particular lush song, "In Passing Years," on repeat. The music put me in a musing, meditative, sometimes wistful state, but not melancholy. I trudged along the sand one afternoon as my playlist randomly brought up Jon Bon Jovi's "You Give Love a Bad Name." I laughed out loud.

Shot through the heart and you're to blame.
You give love a bad name!

What timing. I shouted it out on repeat play for the next ten minutes dancing in the sand, laughing, and singing at the top of my lungs. Even if there had been any other walkers on that deserted beach the waves and wind would have drowned me out. What freedom! After I quit laughing, the heartache came - again.

Later in the summer that year I was invited to the home of friends I think His Nibs and I would have considered our best friends. They lived high up a windy bougainvillea and mountain laurel fringed road in magical Mandeville Canyon near Santa Monica. Our times together over a decade had been warm and intimate, intellectual, soulful, creative, and fun-filled. Going to visit them for the first time as a solo, I wondered how it would impact our conversation, our time and the very essence of being together. We had been such a tight foursome.

At first it was a little awkward. Clearly a leg of the table was missing. After a beautiful gourmet dinner of their favorite black cod and California vegetables, sitting by the woodfire sipping the last of our delicious central coast pinot noir, I raised the question head on.

"Does it feel different being with me as a single person and if so, what does that mean for our continued relationship?" We had always had honest conversations about so many things the question did not feel awkward, unexpected, or intrusive.

Don held his glass by the stem, twirling the remainder of his pour, and said thoughtfully, "Yes, it does for me in some ways I think we will all understand more fully over the years. We love you, of course, for who you are, and we know you love us, and yet the balance feels different."

"And," said Paige, "we want you in our lives and all of us in our lives."

It would be the first of a number of conversations of the awareness of the differences I would experience over the next year or so. The energy of three is intangible and powerful. It is different from the intangible and powerful energy of four. It's the power of shared and common history together of four of us versus with only some of us together. I imagine it's a light version of what widows and widowers experience or any other newly-divorced person peeling off of a couple foundation. I would learn that some repositions work gracefully and others don't. For us, and several other shared friends, it was not a matter of picking sides. Sometimes the result was just attrition, who lived near who and had more contact. It was propinquity, as Zelda, Dobie Gillis' chemistry class partner in the 1960's sitcom *Dobie Gillis* would explain as to how she knew they would end up together. There are some friends I didn't "lose" so much as they just wandered off, wandered off from the "crash site" I guess you could say.

In Mandeville Canyon I awoke early, often barely dawn, and depending on the temperature of fickle southern California mornings, sat in the glass enclosed "Hawaii Room" which looked out into the succulent native garden of plants and trees, shrubs, flowers, and on one memorable morning, a rattlesnake. If the morning was even slightly warmer, I would sit on the stone patio at the small iron bistro table, (now keeping one eye scanning for a snake) and gaze up the steep canyon hillside covered in vines and flowers. My mug of choice on those mornings was a colorful Italian pottery mug, ample, joyful. My long view here went more vertical than horizontal, a view I found, with reflection, to be apt and what I needed. Looking upward at the fruit trees and vines, distant echoes from my Southern Baptist days reminded me of the verse from the Psalmist, "I will lift up mine eyes to the hills from whence cometh my help." And it did come, that help. Every morning. I sat in the early morning mist of the fog that had not yet lifted or burned away, being present, tears, unbidden, would come and my heart felt connected and moving along that slow road towards new wholeness, knowing I had a very long way to go, but grateful for the immediacy of the journey and the many long roads of friendship that nurtured me here. Somehow I knew it would have to be me on the road in this new single role visiting people, keeping connected, and not waiting for others. That was okay for now. I understood I had to be in the forefront so that my friends understood where I "was," how I was feeling, and what I needed. Mandeville Canyon helped me see that clearly.

There were other early mornings over the next months, mornings with good strong coffee in special mugs in Tucson and Boulder, always with a patio or deck giving me a long view to somewhere.

And then there was Meeker Ranch, owned by our friends in our Manor Born neighborhood, five hours west of Boulder, sitting on a high hill amidst other soft gentle hills and overlooking one of the most beautiful valleys I've ever been in. Lush, green, light shifting and playing throughout the day on the mountains from early dawn's glimmer to the lengthening shadows of sunset, embracing the valley, embracing me. The main log house of Meeker Ranch has a large L-shaped covered porch with Adirondack chairs anchoring the long end of the porch. There is enough room for eight or ten people to watch a rainstorm, enjoy a conversation or, as I was inclined to do when not engaged in conversation with my beautiful host Caryn, listen to music, sit and read, or simply sit. During the early morning hours as the sun rose over the hills, my steaming coffee was held in a whimsical ceramic mug bearing the black and white face of an insouciant sheep, reflecting the long history of sheep ranching that sustained the valley for many years. I loved that mug. It was perfect for the time and place in my journey in which I found myself. Solid. The right size. I was beginning to gradually feel some of those things again. Meeker Ranch porch sheltered me when it rained with sudden, hard, crazy, afternoon rain; shaded me during the times of high midday sun; provided a cocoon under a blanket in the cool evening on the summer solstice, gazing at an almost-full moon over the hills. The sturdy Adirondack chairs with their broad arms held hot mugs of coffee in the morning, iced water in the afternoons, and chilled wine in the cool of the evening. Always, there was the long view down to and across the glorious valley.

As the days and nights and visits to places, homes, and friends across the country wore on, and that harsh, unimaginable winter moved into spring and then into summer in the company of Mother Road, I felt immense gratitude for all the beauty and all the friends that were slowly helping me piece myself back together – not into my old life or self – that would never be, or be possible or even desirable, but gradually into a new con-stellation of cells, insights, desires. Tom Stoppard, the English playwright wrote, "Look on every exit being an entrance somewhere else." My car, my seat on the airplane, my many porches and long views, were all taking me to new entrances to somewhere, and were all my traveling hermitage, sacred spaces to think, read, reflect, mourn. More journeys were ahead.

So far the road trip validated that I could still gather my Grit, trust my heart and instincts, and move towards some sphere of light, even if I couldn't see clearly what it was and where it might lead. It was beginning to feel like I would land some-where, and soon. With equal measures of anticipation and trepidation, I wondered where, and how and when I would know.

I began to ask the troubling question, "How did I end up here, at this age, in this situation? Would I ever truly know?"

As the sun set over the hills at Meeker Ranch one last time, I swear I heard the deep, resonant, moving, and sexy voice of Elvis singing across the valley. Yes, I thought. There was, most certainly, on that beautiful evening, Peace in the Valley.

Sing it, Elvis. Oh, sing it.

In Passing Years

Lyrics and Music by Rick Jensen

In passing years it all looks the same
And just the names will change
We all will love too many times, but just the friends remain
And so these things I'll say to you
Over tea for two on a wasted day
When two friends meet and share
I hope that you will still be there.

In passing years we'll speak of truth
    and things we've learned since youth
Youth bears no age only the stage of wants and first embrace
So it is two people meet and they fall in love,
    one strong one weak
But it's still clear they must contend with honesty
To find an end.

Some endings glad, some endings sad
Some strong but most are weak
We'll sit with ours in a closing bar
No games, just friends remain.

And so these things I say to you
Over tea for two on a wasted day
When two friends meet and share
I hope that you will still be there.

Reckoning

5 – It Will Be Forever…Or Maybe Not

"We are here to ruin ourselves and to break our hearts and love the wrong people and die."

~ Nicholas Cage in *Moonstruck*

"How shall my heart be reconciled to its feast of losses?"

~ Stanley Kunitz *The Layers*

I will never know what it feels like to "fall in love forever," as the old song goes.

When I fall in love it will be forever,
Or I'll never fall in love.

Too late for that, I guess. The halfway point to forever blew past me about thirty years ago. Okay. More.

I arrived in the beautiful Texas Hill Country two marriages and divorces down and a third divorce, at the age of sixty-four, staring me in the eye with its knowing smirk. Me, of all people. Me, who when asked in my personal interview before the panel of judges as a finalist in the 1969 Miss Lubbock Contest what I wanted to do with my life answered, "My highest aspiration is to be a good Christian wife and mother." *That* mark flew by me by a country mile in only a few short years. Me, who decided at an early age to "save myself" for marriage for that "special someone" God would choose for me at the right time.

But three? Three-peater? Three-time loser? Ouch. I never dreamed I would be the one to be such a cautionary tale of loser womanhood by my own estimation, as well as my family and the entire Southern Baptist convention, all of which trained me for marriage – the fall in love forever kind. God either can't count or has a sadistic sense of humor.

I remember being fourteen years old and reciting from memory verses from Proverbs 31 of the Old Testament of the Bible. Checking off that box of memory work was an important step on the list of requirements to achieve Queen Regent status in the Girls' Auxiliary ranks of the Southern Baptist Church. GA's (as we were called)—sort of a Girl Scout meets Princess Leia or the Bride of Jesus, or something like that. We started young – around nine – much like the Brownie ranks of the Girl Scouts, spending hours filling in and checking off the requirements to earn the badges and recognition of our accomplishments, which in my case were the various geometric components made of felt, comprising a special symbol.

"Who can find a virtuous woman, for her price is far above rubies?" (Proverbs 31:10) I'm thinking, that's probably me, right? Virtuous. My price is far above rubies, for sure. Looking back, I might have asked "What *is* virtue for a twelve- or thirteen-year-old?" Or, "What's the actual going price for rubies these days?" I should have done some research I guess, but then, I was young. Starting at nine I decided to pursue this years-long trek through the GA steps toward the ultimate attainment of Queen Regent status, an unconscious precursor to my PhD path to root out knowledge and achieve the prize for myself and for others to admire.

The first step on this pilgrimage was to achieve the status of Maiden. Maiden. Like little Bo Peep or Robin Hood's Maid Marian? At nine, I didn't even know what the questions were, such as, "What *is* a 'Maiden'?" Or even, "Why should I want to be one?" Achieving the status of Maiden required memorizing simple Bible verses and answering simple questions about the Bible. The award was a plain green felt octagon six inches wide representing Growth.

Second Level, Lady-in-Waiting, was awarded the following year and was a gold felt octagon border about ½" or ¾" representing Purity. (Purity!!) I am eleven years old at this point… pure in heart? Pure for Jesus?

Third Level was Princess. Finally, something I could understand and identify with. The symbol of achievement for Princess was a white felt star for the middle of the octagon with the letters GA in gold felt. Gold for Sincerity. It didn't feel like much recognition or reward for all that work to be a Princess. More Bible verse memorization and other tasks I don't remember.

At last, Queen. Ah, yes. The symbol for Queen was a flimsy paper or thin cardboard embossed gold crown, an absolute dead ringer for the Burger King gold paper crown passed through the drive-in window years later by indifferent, spotty-faced teenagers. The coronation of the crown occurred in the annual "Presentation Ceremony" for all of us in long white dresses in which our annual accomplishments were recognized in a special ceremony on a mid-week evening in May in Trinity Baptist Church in San Antonio, or dozens of similar sanctuaries big and small across the Southern Baptist Convention. We knelt to receive our crown, from whom I don't remember. All of us, to a girl, in that Texas church sanctuary, even at that age, knew our kneeling was not remotely up there status-wise with the more widely known and admired deep curtsy known as the Dallas Debutante Dip, but it was, to all of us anyway, extremely important and, even better, imbued with spiritual grace and not just worldly glamor.

The Girls' Auxiliary and the progressive steps of accomplishment in the faith represented a trajectory of young Christian womanhood towards steady spiritual ascension. I can still picture in my mind's eye how I practiced kneeling for my crown the day after I received my Princess star. I realize looking back I always possessed the gift of personal manifestation of my dreams and visions. Desire it. Think it. Picture it. Do it. It has served me well. When I look at the 8 X 10 black and white photos taken by the church photographer and sold with the familiar pressured carnival hawking of school photos, I find a certain level of discomfort and dis-ease at the sight of the cluster of prepubescent and young adolescent girls dressed up like young brides, representing Purity no less. My younger brother, probably five or six at the time, was my crown bearer walking down the aisle in his little white shirt and white sports coat, black clip-on bow tie and black pants, carrying the white satin pillow to which the precious crown was pinned.

A year later, after receiving my crown, I earned my wooden gold painted scepter to recognize my increasing status in God's eyes as Queen-With-A-Scepter. It felt anti-climactic after all the queenly hoopla. I attained the green satin cape lined with white satin and tied at the neck with a tasseled gold cord as Queen Regent. To achieve this status I had to make a 3-foot by 3-foot cross-stitch map of the world among other things. Yes, the world, for God's sake (literally). I had almost finished it after more than a year of weekend slumber parties with GA friends who were also on the same track, when my friend Barbara spilled a bottle of Texas' legendary Big Red soda on it. They don't call it Big Red for nothing. I wanted to kill her, but I didn't think I would have been awarded the coveted green and white satin cape if I had blood on my hands or on the blemished world map. Maybe I could have passed that off too as Big Red, who knows?

The evening of The Big Spill was also the Friday night after JFK's assassination in Dallas that afternoon. Emotions ran high. It wasn't the last time the intersection of different events, globally and personally, would meet head on in my world with tears that engulfed it all with no particular discrimination. Just sorrow and tears. For reasons we had no way to understand, living in Texas felt like Texas was responsible in some way for our president's death. For several years after, it was hard to admit to anyone I lived in Texas because their first reaction or response was about Dallas and the president's assassination. As I look back now I think that was probably the first time I felt tarnished or shamed being associated with Texas, because I called Texas home.

More than thirty years later I was in a residential intensive as part of my academic work in human and organization development. Long, late night conversations reminiscent of under-graduate all-night dorm sessions took us deep into our childhood memories with confessions of sexual exploitations, religious quests and questioning of everything in general, the whole cathartic, introspective, self-revelatory ball of wax. During one of these conversations a grad-student colleague and I discovered we had both been GA's, I, achieving the highest order of Queen Regent, of course, and Libby, beautiful, elegant, gentle, southern belle, accomplished and brilliant Libby from Atlanta, that of Queen. We both told stories to the group in the dorm room with genuine pride, affection, and nostalgia, mixed with our scholarly adult ironic perspective, of course, between bites of Cracker Jack®, peanut butter stuffed pretzels, and hits of box white and red wine, along with an above-it-all soupcon of mild derision about kneeling to receive our crowns. I stood up and reenacted the exact moment of coronation, kneeling and bowing my head to the amusement of my increasingly tipsy friends.

"After all these years" I confessed, "Even after several marriages and divorces and many cross-country moves, I still have that creased tacky thin piece of gold cardboard that is my crown."

"I don't have mine anymore," Libby said matter of factly. "It was stripped from me by the pastor of my church when he came to see me in the hospital where I had just given birth as an unwed teenage mother." Libby began to cry, tears, I suppose, triggered by the complicated layered memories of hurt, shame, and anger she still carried and had buried until those memories of remembering the pride of kneeling for that crown reclaimed her for a few seconds. At that moment I hatched a plan. I knew what I had to do.

The next year at the same yearly residential doctoral intensive, the same predictable late-night sessions started up again. One evening I marshaled a dozen of our friends and shared the plan. We agreed to meet late that evening in my room, but I told Libby it was going to be a half hour later than I told the others. In that half hour, I briefed them on the plan.

That evening Libby knocked on the door and let herself in, standing, stunned, in the door frame. My friends and I had formed two lines making a long V with me at the head. I began singing the Girls Auxiliary Hymn, "We've a Story to Tell To the Nations," as the others hummed along. Apparently, I have a core competency giving crash hymn singing/humming courses. Libby looked at me holding the flimsy gold crown and knew instantly what was coming. Walking between the two lines toward me, Libby dropped to her knees.

"I crown you – again – Queen Libby of the Girls Auxiliary," I said, placing the worn piece of cardboard I had carried cross

country with me over thirty years on her head. Libby threw
both arms around my knees, leaving two mascara tear-stained
circles on one knee of my white linen summer slacks. Only
holding her for as long as she needed and wanted to be held
quieted her heart. Only breaking out the box white wine which
was already chilling in the room refrigerator quieted her tears.

Why had I kept the crown all those years? What did it mean to
me? Some deeply-buried desire to attain an unattainable vision of
womanhood? Would having it make me worthy of those rubies
– at any price? How could it matter thirty years later to a
"museum quality left-leaning Unitarian Liberal Democrat," as
the raconteur and writer Garrison Keillor once described
himself when someone questioned what it was like to present
his live radio show *Prairie Home Companion* in Dallas? Could it
possibly be so that I would have it at this very moment to pass
on to sweet Libby? Or did I need it for other reasons?

As I think about that evening in the hotel room with adult
women in their forties, fifties, and even sixties, I am amazed at
the powerful vice-like grip of the past, the spiritual presences
that both nourish and inflame us, those early profound experiences that shape our lives and stay deeply embedded in our
hearts and memories, even when their voices are quiet whispers
and not angry shouts. They are there. The greasy residue of
shame is hard to wash away, scrub away, wish away, or even
pray away. I realized that evening that even though I had
successfully and expertly navigated the waters of avoiding
shameful teenage pregnancy myself in the 60s, my own layers
of shame had accumulated over many years with each failed
relationship, each failed attempt to lasso that emotional unicorn
of perfect womanhood, that Virtuous Woman I had been led to
believe was real and out there and attainable if I were just good
enough to fall in love the right way, forever. Someone, surely,

would pony up at least a couple rubies to prove my worth, meager as it might be.

Today when I remember that evening with a heartbroken woman and her memory of being stripped of a flimsy bit of cardboard that meant so much to her, a flimsy bit of cardboard coloring her sense of worth for decades, it reminds me there is more than one way to express Purity and Sincerity, if they need to be expressed at all, all of them of higher value and virtue than the tissue thin caricature of my early Southern Baptist teachings. I'll take my older adult version any day. Daddy used to tell us kids, "There's nothing deader than the past." He was wrong about that. In contrast the Irish say, "The thing about the past is…it's not the past." They are right about that. I was about to find out at this time in my life of The Great Shitstorm that Daddy was wrong about the past being dead in more ways than I dreamed possible.

When I moved to Texas, the Year of the Great Shitstorm, I still carried that shame of three failed marriages, a virtual billboard to failure of being a virtuous woman. My "story," as most people still believe, because it's what I told them, was I left my successful, glamorous life in NYC and moved back to Texas after my mother's death to be with my precious Daddy, suffering from rapidly increasing dementia in his final days. I wanted to be with him as long as he still knew me, the story went. I know now as I knew even then it wasn't the whole story, the whole truth. To this day, a decade later, no more than a handful of people in my small artsy town know anything about the shadow backstory that brought me here. One of the first things I learned about songwriting when I got to Texas is the one and only true maxim that all it takes to write a song is three chords and the truth. Maybe it was time for me to come out of the shadows of three husbands with the truth.

Three strikes and I was out. Out of my beautiful home in Connecticut and the life I deeply loved. Out of the cabaret spotlight in New York City. Out of the game of love and happiness and, certainly, out of the comfort, safety, and respectability of love "forever." I had to reinvent, recalibrate, reorient myself. I told myself the very personal part of my story was nobody's business. As I look back now on that year, I realize I needed to continue to uphold a certain image of myself even in this re-creation and re-birthing event. Find a ruby, lose a ruby. Leading with my story about myself with three marriages and divorces seemed hardly the best way to create a new life, especially in Texas where football games, Lions Club meetings, and Harvest Moon Dances still begin with a prayer ending, "in Jesus' name," especially when echoes of Jesus admonishing The Woman at The Well for all her husbands were freshly rico-cheting around in my brain. While Jesus did say to the woman, "It's okay, honey," or something like that, he still specifically referred to her five husbands and the man she was currently with who was not her husband. So, let's face it. He *was* keeping count. I felt he was talking to me, give or take a couple husbands.

As I looked around, everyone I saw had apparently achieved that "happy ever after." I met more couples my first year back in Texas who married right out of college and were still married, now celebrating forty and fifty year anniversaries, than I met in my combined forty-three years outside of Texas. Something completely new to me, many of them seemed quite happy and still committed; with children, most of whom were raised and out the door and successful in the adult world; grandchildren who adored their grandparents and grandparents who doted on them. Fantastically enough, some of those couples I'd even gone to high school with. Some of them were married to the ones they dated in high school. High School! I *knew* these couples but hadn't seen their like for most of the years I was outside of Texas. Here I stood. The outlier. The embodiment of shame and failure. Not worth a single ruby. No one needed to know. I felt like a catfish out of water in this Texas world.

Part of me knew deep down I would feel this way if I came back. After an entire adult lifetime, I had changed. Some things had changed in Texas, but a lot hadn't. For instance, after not even thinking about college football in forty-three years, it only took a few months to get right back into gear with university rivalries, school songs, mascots, and Saturday afternoons spent watching bodies and colors and pompoms racing up and down a familiar field in unfamiliar, vastly upgraded stadiums.

The local accents were startling and jarring and unpleasant to listen to, and to this day many of them still are, but it didn't take long for me to click into words and phrases embedded in my past. My mother, in particular, had picked up inflections, questionable word choices, and phrasings that grated when she spoke them. I often had to quiet my internal judgments about the person speaking the words when they landed on my ears. Years later I look around and wonder how many others I know in my small community of retired executives-turned-artists were reinventing, recrafting, and rewriting their own stories. It is a community ideally suited for that. I suspect we are all keeping secrets.

It didn't help, of course, several years later when I learned that according to a recent census only three percent of women have been divorced three times. It seemed beyond the realm of coincidence that of the six women in my tight circle of Diva Girlfriends in Connecticut, three of us were married (and two of us subsequently divorced, one divorced twice and then widowed) three times. I did not feel like a fish out of water all those years outside of Texas. In my world living and working in New York City, traveling internationally, wining and dining at the best watering holes and restaurants, friends were having affairs with their therapists, their colleagues, their trainers, their professors, sometimes with each other. I threw my hat in that ring a time or two myself. I could have conveniently gone down to 47th Street and 6th Avenue in New York City (known as Diamond Ally) and cashed in a couple of rubies, but I didn't have any left. If I were ever going to be an asset to any man again, it wasn't going to be because of any backstock in precious gems.

Once I was back in Texas I was a single woman in my sixties in a community of cozy couples. I felt as exposed as a coffee stain on a white linen shirt on one hand, and as impenetrable as a blank slate on the other. I'd always believed I would end up like those friends I admired if I found the right partner. There would be a click of souls snapping into place, like the pop beads on necklaces from my childhood. I thought I had found that connection but I was wrong. Three times.

Texas dance halls have it right. I realize that in every New York City cabaret show I did, there was a song by a Texas singer-songwriter. Most of the time I did not realize they were Texas singer-songwriters until I moved back to Texas. I've been a lifelong song collector and with cabaret I became an intentional song hunter. I came across "Baby Took a Limo to Memphis" about thirty years ago on a CD compilation compiled by an author I follow and admire, and loved the sassiness of it. I'd never heard of Guy Clark. Who was Guy Clark? Returning to Texas I've learned he is one of the best known, most iconic musicians of this century. At the time, I only knew he wrote a song that fit the narrative arc of my very first NYC show. Later,

on another CD compilation, I heard Caroline Herring's "Texas
Two-Step" which fit beautifully in another show:

Central Texas and the Hill Country are dotted with many dance
halls, wooden structures often going back a century or more
and a close cousin in spirit to Irish pubs. I began to venture out
to some of them. Couples young and old scooted across the
floor. Friendly looking groups sat on the sidelines watching and
talking over cold beers. A few grandfathers danced with their
small granddaughters firmly on their shoe tops, and always the
sweet, addictive slow-slow, quick-quick playing the seductive
siren call to the dance floor.

Couples who have two-stepped together for half a century
move as one in the line of dance, usually nothing fancy, but
always in perfect sync, including the every-so-often close to the
body perfectly executed twirl. You can tell they have done these
moves a thousand times. In my mind nothing quite matches in
words the testimony to a long term relationship than a couple
dancing together in any kind of dance, but there's something
about watching couples two-step that speaks to commitment,
devotion, and history, or perhaps I'm just loading all of that on
them out of my own need.

Not long after moving to Wimberley and creating my band the
Cashmere Cowgirls, we three women of the band decided to go
dancing at Mercer Street Dance Hall in Dripping Springs, about
twenty minutes away along winding Ranch Road 12, the back-
bone between several small towns in the Hill Country. It

was an occasion to get dolled up in some western gear or flowy dresses and boots and join in for the hour-long lesson at the beginning of the evening, taught for a decade by John and Twozee Luper, former Western Dance National Champions, now retired and raising llamas and a couple of mean peacocks on their ranch in Blanco. After the lesson we planned to sit and watch the fun happening on the dance floor, lean against the railing from our wooden bench front row seats, listen to the band, and have a couple glasses of wine or a couple cold beers. It was going to be a swell evening.

We thought we were going to get away with a half-assed hour of giggling during the lesson. We were wrong. John Luper told us that by the end of the hour we would be able to get out on the dance floor and actually dance and have a good time. He and Twozee taught us the minimum required steps and dance protocol to the soundtrack of Johnny Lee "Looking for Love" out of the Urban Cowboy movie playing out through the boombox.

Everyone needed a partner for the lesson. We were a couple of guys short. John pleasantly strong armed some of the men standing outside the dance floor who'd come early for a beer or two, and perhaps to be strong armed for precisely that reason. John was right. This was no Urban Cowboy fantasy dance hall and John and Twozee Luper would not allow us to be pretend two-steppers. After an hour of no nonsense focus, we were scooting around in the large counterclockwise line of dance with little effort and amazingly few toes crushed by or on our fancy boots. The lesson ended. We made our contributions to John and Twozee's "Taco Breakfast Tip Jar." We grabbed our primo seats next to the railing around the dance floor.

The band playing that night had already set up and completed sound check, so with only a few minutes between the time we finished our last quick-quick, slow-slow, the band kicked up with the heavy downbeats on the one and three. Dancers streamed out on the floor. Young couples; old couples; tourists (you can always tell); hot shot cowboys, but mostly ordinary guys in collared or western shirts, many with hats; hot stuff young women in slip dresses, hats and boots; and the marrieds (you can always tell).

About four bars into the music, a tall, skinny guy in a red cowboy shirt and tight jeans covering his long skinny legs came over to us sitting by the railing, tapped me on the shoulder and offered his hand. Wordless, I followed him out on the dance floor, we got into the line of dance, and away we went.

It was a fast two-step so we were clocking around the hall. He dipped me. He twirled me. He dipped me again. But John and Twozee Luper were right. I hung in there (barely) and was returned to my seat by the gentleman with a "thank you." Off he went to get a beer or another partner. My two girlfriends had the same experience. It went on throughout the evening, dancing with different partners, circling around with previous ones, until the band took a break. I was breathless, sweaty, and ecstatic. My fears of coming with other women and having to sit everything out because there was no one to dance with, or conversely, being hounded and harassed because I was there as a single woman, were 1000% unfounded. The song was right. "We only came here to dance." We managed to take a breather during the band's break and caught up with a couple of glasses of surprisingly top shelf chardonnay. We danced as long as we could before closing up the dance floor for the night and headed home.

Dance halls became a regular feature for me. Evenings combined all the finest elements of life – dressing up with great clothes; stunning jewelry; awesome boots; fun with good girlfriend company and live music; meeting new people both men and women; and soaking in the authentic Hill Country vibe of Texas two-stepping. And I could do it again tomorrow night. Or next week. Or whenever I wanted to. I could come by myself or with a group. This was a real part of my new community. No one in the worlds I had left on either coast would have understood it. I barely did. I briefly tried to picture His Nibs in boots learning to two-step. The image just wasn't coming to me. If I weren't in a relationship at all, and I wasn't tracking on the Forever track, I was going to have a great time doing things I'd never considered or known about or thought I'd ever want to do. The tradeoff for Forever, even if I hadn't wanted it or planned it, for now, was not bad.

When I was in the second grade at Fort Sam Houston Elementary School in San Antonio, the teacher divided the class into three reading groups: The Cardinals, the Blue Birds, and the Sparrows. We all knew who was who. I knew from the get-go that the Cardinals, my group, were the fast readers and the Sparrows, well…they were Sparrows. I wish somewhere along the way someone had done the same when I was beginning to find my way in the world of love and marriage. If someone had taken me aside and said, "Honey, I might as well tell you this now. When it comes to love and forever, you're a Sparrow." I might not have liked it but at least I'd know what to expect and make sure my plans included two-stepping from the start.

His Eye Is on the Sparrow

Lyrics Mrs. C. D. Martin, Music by Chas. H. Gabriel, 1905

Why should I feel discouraged?
Why should the shadows fall?
Why should my heart grow weary
And long for heaven and home?
When Jesus is my portion
My constant friend is He
His eye is on the sparrow
And I know he watches me.
His eye is on the sparrow.
And I know he watches me

I sing because I'm happy
I sing because I'm free.
For his eye is on the sparrow
And I know he watches me.

Whenever I am tempted
Whenever clouds arise
When songs give place to sighing
When hope within me dies
I draw the closer to Him
From care he sets me free
His eye is on the Sparrow
And I know he watches me

6 – Rethinking Resiliency

"What Becomes of the Broken-Hearted?"
Song by Jimmy Ruffin
Motown Records Soul Label, 1969

Where does our need for reconciliation with dashed dreams come from? How does it begin? I'm not talking about forgiveness, rather the small impulses of recognition that tell us we need to move on?

"You're a strong woman, maybe the strongest I know. You'll get over this," said my friend over cups of strong black Guatemalan coffee at our favorite beachside café in Santa Barbara. It was four months after the day of double heartbreak and I was back in Santa Barbara attending to some academic and personal business. My strategy to hit the road seemed to have been a pretty good one. My time with friends in out-of-the-usual locations had been healing. New scenery, imagery and conversations helped me get out of my usual patterns with no expectations of an agenda or "moving on." What did I expect from myself of moving on? What would that look like? How would I know?

Half-listening to my friend, my gaze was on the dolphins just offshore, dipping in and out of the shallow surf. Other Santa Barbarians around us were focused on beachside pancakes, omelets, or a mimosa or two, which were starting to feel like a good idea and a missed opportunity. The words had come from a good friend and I know she thought she was being supportive.

"You're going to be stronger than ever, better than ever, when you come through this." Honestly, what else was she going to say? Yes, I did believe that would be true, eventually, and that's a good thing. For the first few months of that awful rupture in my life I wasn't sure I wanted to come through it. I had to figure out a strategy for staying put and moving on or at least through. I didn't have much emotional energy for the task, but I had to try, I knew, since I'd made the decision to do it.

I am often surprised at the threads of life unspooling from experiences from years before, surfacing at unexpected moments to be just what I need at the time. On the surface there doesn't seem to be a connection, but with hindsight they turn into something new that can, if I listen to them and sit still long enough, allow me to make some different connections, other decisions. Gazing at the dolphins that Santa Barbara morning several months after my Double Barreled Heartbreak, an experience from a dozen years before softly dove and surfaced as well, taking me across the Atlantic in my mind, back to a tiny village in the south of France and a centuries old stone farmhouse with a brand new pool where His Nibs and I had negotiated a home exchange for three weeks.

Our eager expectations of this experience collided immediately with our growing daily reality. It didn't take long to realize we were in the middle of the deadliest heatwave to hit Europe since 1540. The European death toll that summer would eventually reach 35,000. Fifteen thousand deaths in France alone, many in the cities, elderly left alone while children and siblings fled to cooler places, usually with little success. A shameful footnote to that time, scarcely commented on. So began our home exchange.

The stone farmhouse did not have air conditioning, of course, or "salon climatasse," which apparently translated from French means "really, really weak ineffective lukewarm air conditioning." All the bedrooms in the farmhouse were on the second floor. Heat rises. The windows were quite small given the period they were built. For most of the house's three-hundred-year history the thick walls and small windows probably were effective enough for maintaining heat in the winter and cool in the summers. But not for us. Not then. Breathing was difficult. Putting on any clothes at all required a conscious decision every morning to eschew blatant nudism which, even though we were in France, seemed only a moderately compelling idea but an idea at that. I tossed and turned all night, every night, finally getting up around 5:00 as dawn was breaking, headed downstairs, and without stopping walked out to the pool, fell in, and stayed there. Not swimming, not floating on any silly inflatable swan or, God forbid, neon noodle, just standing there in the pool with the water up to my neck. Occasionally I'd step out and get my book and try to read without success, falling into the pool again. Talking seemed too much effort. At some point I'd go into the house and throw some breakfast together – croissants, fruit, occasionally an egg. Turning on the stove was not worth the monumental effort required because then we'd have to stand over it and do something to whatever we were torturing with additional heat, and that would be us, mostly.

By evening, as the sun would start to set over the beautiful hills, we'd pile into the decrepit Volvo station wagon that was provided with our exchange home, drive the twenty minutes into the closest town, breathing and soaking in the car's air conditioning, weak as it was. Sometimes we'd just drive around for an hour with no destination in mind or reason to get out of the car. Once we chanced upon a small village fair and had a few rounds with the bumper cars, if only for sheer distraction from the breezeless night. We cackled maniacally as we rammed into each other's cars, momentarily forgetting the heat. Some evenings we'd find a place for a beautiful open-air dinner hoping for a breeze along with the wine, and then drive home, dreading our arrival, climbing the narrow stone steps to our respective room-size ovens after one long, last dip in the pool, only to lie awake all night in the oppressive heat and stillness and "get up and do it again," as Jackson Browne would sing. How were we going to survive?

Seven days into this enervating experience, we decided it would be a good idea to drive to Bordeaux, book a hotel, and at least have some sputtering intermittent comfort with *salon climatasse*. We lethargically mumbled to each other a few things about seeing some sights and exploring the city, mainly because I think that's what we thought we were expected to say. In our Rick Steves regional tour Bible we located a small, contemporary, boutique hotel centrally located in the City Centre of Bordeaux. Frankly, all we cared about was that it said it had AC. I was in the middle of a 1500-page intergenerational family saga of some kind. The heat was so oppressive I can't even tell you what the book was now — very unlike me. I listlessly threw the book and a change of clothes into a small bag and we sputtered off in the ancient Volvo.

The hotel was delightful. In addition to being small, it had a cinema noir theme to it. Every room, hallway, and lobby had huge, oddly refreshingly cooling, black and white movie poster size photos of film stars and movie cuts, mostly from the French and American classic cinema noir era of the '30s, '40s, and '50s. Posters from Alfred Hitchcock's *Strangers on a Train,*

Les Diaboliques, and *The Big Sleep* appeared in sleeping rooms, elevators, and the bar. It was completely charming with one exception. The *salon climatasse* barely chugged along, its presence detectable, but almost imperceptibly so. Never mind. I found my comfy chair and reading lamp in the bedroom and settled in. I would accept whatever the AC goddess was offering and be grateful.

Twenty minutes later His Nibs was standing before me, sweat already glistening on his upper lip, man bag on his shoulder, maps in hand. "Let's go and explore the city, I'm ready."

I looked up with my best dismissive, disdainful French-like one arched eyebrow look and said, "No, I'm not budging. You have a good time," so unlike me as I'm usually the first one out the door. After he left, I sat in the chair reading, snoozing, happily soaking up what little AC there was and somewhat shamefaced to admit I was grateful not having to share any of it. Hours later he returned, soaked with sweat, but pleasantly excited (in my mind disproportionately so) about his excursion into the city. I never saw anything of the city of Bordeaux, which at the time was totally dug up and under construction in every square block and roadway of it, so I rationalized I wouldn't have seen anything anyway that day.

Even in my heat desperation I could not pass up a day of touring some of the famous vineyards, however. The heat was over 100 degree F. (37 degrees Celsius for the Francophile purists, and there's always one between the covers of any book.) We left early in the morning in our feebly air-conditioned tour bus, dreading the moment we'd arrive at another exquisitely beautiful vineyard, climb off the bus and walk the dusty roads, sometimes sweating up a hill, to listen to a lecture about terroir and distinctions of grapes grown on various types of hillsides.

Most of us were too heat stunned and desperate for another water to have the words and stories sink in. We sprinted from shade tree to shade tree where shade was available, praying there was a cool ancient stone cellar somewhere on our itinerary.

As the day progressed, we managed to get out of our heads consumed with our own sorry personal situation long enough to wonder if *we* were this uncomfortable, wilting, desperately thirsty all day, how were the grapes doing? How were the vineyards experiencing this epic heatwave? What did it mean to *them?* Was this going to permanently destroy hundreds of years and multi-generations of family vineyard cultivation, or at the very least damage them for years to come? We began to rouse from our heat induced stupors to start asking questions of our guides. Were we facing collective vineyard decimation for years to come resulting in skyrocketing wine prices and wine short-ages? How could we not be? The blistering heat wave had already lasted several weeks and was heading into several more.

The answers were surprising. Repeatedly we were reassured that the roots of these ancient vines go down deep, finding the water that is far below the surface. We didn't need to worry about them. I found that hard to understand but given the lushness of the leaves all around us, and the still blooming single rose at the end of every vine row, the one that repelled pests or became the canary in the mine symbol of some pest or rot occurring down the row, a tradition that has gone on for centuries despite the weeks of tortuous heat and dryness, I decided to believe.

A song, "*All The Roots Grow Deeper When It's Dry,*" by the singer-songwriter David Wilcox, a friend and songwriter I've been a fan of for decades, came to mind. I'd listened to the song for

years, but that day I drank in the lyrics in a new and deeper way,
as if they were a drink of cool water;

Exactly a decade later that experience with the vineyards and
that song came to mind as I was in the midst of the first wave
of shell shock from The Great Shit Storm. As I tried to stay
present in the emotional pain of those weeks and months,
wondering if I could or would survive, or even if I wanted to, I
thought of those vineyards reaching down to find the water
with no prodding or help from me or anyone else. They sought
that deep, cool place naturally, effortlessly, which in my world
translated into friends and colleagues and family I'd never
known before being in the helpless space I was in now. I never
knew how far down I could reach and still be watered and
nourished because I'd never needed to go that deep before and
had never known the possibility existed.

The vineyards, of course, were deeply resilient and over the
years came back stronger. I have come to believe that resilience,
as I have always defined it – as "bouncing back" – is overrated.
I acknowledge my temptation, and that of almost everyone I
know, to achieve the state of some sort of equilibrium as
quickly as possible, sometimes dismissively called "moving on
with your life."

During those dark days it seemed there existed an external
metric, the visual marker my friends were hoping to identify any
day now. "You're strong. You'll get through this." Another way
of calling out my "grit?" "You're going to be stronger than ever,

better than ever when you come through this." And yes, I did believe that would be true, eventually, and that's a good thing. I knew I was strong.

"Pick yourself up, brush yourself off, and start all over again," was the refrain from a childhood song my mother use to sing around the house. I'm tired of picking up pieces and reconfiguring them into a new me. It wasn't that I was in my sixties and getting divorced for the third time. I'm not that unique. The generational phenomenon has become so significant it has its own demographic label: Silver Splitters.[7] For a third time I was accumulating additional complicated family relationships to throw into the Mixmaster, in with those already gone before. My hurt was tangled up in the realization of my aging in the middle of this latest failure. Vulnerability weighed heavily as the reality of no parents, no biological children, aging friends with their own vulnerabilities, and two siblings, both without children as well. I'm the object of another new cultural label: Kinless Seniors.[8]

In our country where every major disaster or collective trauma is quickly followed by a rallying cry of "they/that won't get us down!" "We will rebuild immediately bigger and better," the resilient fighting American Spirit is the stuff of our legend. So, we clear wreckage, bulldoze lots, find new partners, bail the water from the basements, lose weight, dive into our work once again and even deeper – and move on. But what about the lessons I learned from staying in or at least very near the initial wreckage? It all made me feel weary of spirit, tired of rising from the ashes. My Phoenix wings were losing feathers with each reinvention and were beginning to feel a little threadbare and scruffy. What *if* I stayed open in the muck for a while, sat with it, and learned from it? What patience would be required for that?

The Taoist Master Lao Tzu wrote:

> *Do you have the patience to wait*
> *till your mud settles and the water is clear?*
> *Can you remain unmoving*
> *till the right action arises by itself?*

Waiting in the mud does sound suspiciously like wallowing,[9] I must admit. What a great word wallowing.

No, not that kind of wallowing. What I'm talking about is staying open to the emotions if they need to be kept open, not allowing them to recede or, in musical terms, "resolve" too early, not letting them off the hook, so to speak, just to avoid the heaviness of continuing to acknowledge them in my life. The temptation, as well as the goal, I've heard, is to put it all behind me as quickly as possible and move on. The singer-songwriter Gretchen Peters reminded me of the truth of this many years later when I heard her beautiful song, "The Only Cure For the Pain is Pain." How I so wanted that to not be true. I wanted to pay my pain dues, get my receipt stamped Paid in Full, along with the new life that would automatically be handed to me along with the proof of purchase, and just be done.

When my mother was in her last few days in the hospital and then hospice, and Daddy was by her side every minute, he would say to me every few minutes, "It's taking Mama longer to bounce back from this one. You know, she always bounces back. Even if this is taking a little longer than usual, she'll bounce back." Hours before her passing, as he and I sat together in their small, comfortable living room just off their bedroom he asked me, "What do you think about how Mama's doing?" I took his hand, which I often did, and said softly, "Daddy, she's not going to bounce back from this one. I'm sorry." He was quiet.

In the first few months of my own pain, when the metric on a good day was simply breathing in and out long enough to keep my heart pumping, my focus was not on resilience and bouncing back, but physical survival hour to hour. It's when the pain and grief began to age (and what's the metric for that? Like a good steak or fine wine? Like a bad piece of salmon?) I resolved I would impose a "shelf life" on my pain and start showing signs of recovery, of getting on with it, of facing my loss with – yep – Grit. This is what my friends needed to see from me for their own comfort level, to reduce their own anxiety. But what the hell did that look like to me, to them, each of them with different expectations, probably not even realizing they carried expectations? They do. We all do.

In staying attentive to my own wild, free-range grief careening back and forth and up and down several times a day in multiple directions, I began to understand the gift of holding the space and being in the space, feeling all of it. I had a fear that I would shut down too quickly, "bounce back," exercise resilience and Grit. I feared the space in which I was beginning to listen and write in a way I never had before would close too quickly and be gone, like those black worm holes on Star Trek where once the galaxy closed the Starship Enterprise and its passengers would never again have access. I knew I couldn't stay in that space forever, nor did I want to, nor would I survive it. I wanted to find a way to move on, bounce back, and keep the aperture open just a little, just wide enough for me to still glimpse the things I saw and feel the feelings I felt. I wanted to stay open enough for me to keep my "trusting heart" as Jon Kabat-Zinn describes it, in tune with my intuition and spirit. I wasn't consciously aware at the time, but perhaps intuitively I was, that the Road Trip would prove to be one way – a good way – to keep the aperture open.

One day I was talking to a colleague about the roller coaster of emotions around grief, the up and down and spaced out aspects. He offered an observation:

"You know how you're walking across town in New York City, like on 22nd Street, on a really bitter cold and windy day, and you're bundled up completely from head to toe with earmuffs, knitted hat, stocking cap over your face, wool muffler, two pairs of leggings and gloves, and fleece lined boots, bent over against the wind, and you think, if I can just make it to the corner I'll be okay? But when you get there, that corner happens to be Fifth Avenue and a blast of wind you never expected whips and smacks you so hard it lifts your feet off the ground. That's what grief is like. You're going along day to day and it's really hard, but you think you see a little break ahead and you start to feel a little hope - then WHAM!"

In my months of wandering I found I was most susceptible to touching my grief in the early morning hours, dawn, when I was permeable, defenseless, before the day had been strapped on. I was open through meditation or the closeness of thoughts, memories, questions with no answers. I found myself experiencing new waves of grief over the loss of my mother, the loss of my marriage, and, sometimes, because the door to grief was already pried open, to old losses, unresolved endings, and other painful episodes that elbowed their way in.

Sometimes it was a song that triggered the wave, sometimes a specific memory. Sometimes it was a poem, a quilt square, a piece of jewelry, a scent in the air, a long-forgotten note discovered in a book. Sometimes it was a touch. Sometimes an act of kindness out of nowhere. I never knew when it would strike, how long it would last, or how to make it go away. I couldn't. So, I sat with it. Sat in it. Let it wash over me, and then, at some point, like the fog in the Carl Sandberg poem, it moved on. For a while. I felt every cell in my body when grief struck. As painful as it was, it reminded me I was still here, still working to stay alive, and that this was the work I must continue to do. Being ambushed and tackled to the ground by grief helped me continue the work of grieving, knowing in some cases it is probably a lifelong process. Some are smaller griefs. Others are too enormous for words.

Looking back years later I still grieve my mother, my marriage, the loss of a home, of a way of being in the world that I thought would last and didn't. Deciding not to "work through" my grief, but rather hold it, be in it, honor it, deal with the ambushes and sudden, cold blustery blasts as they came at me, dig down as deep as I could in the vineyards of seeming drought, I am grateful I breathed them in and recognized they are all a part of being human and having love in my life. The gift of grief is to remind me that I am alive, and I have had goodness and love in my life worth grieving, and will again, I expect. It is Good Grief after all.

In my mid-20s Daddy gave me the 1952 Zeiss Icon single-fixed-lens camera he'd bought when we lived in Germany in the early fifties. Nothing was automatic of course, so I quickly learned the function of the aperture. The smaller the aperture, the clearer the focus became of a narrow, specific area or subject. That's how those early weeks and months unrolled. Each morning, immediately upon waking after little or no real sleep, I'd make my sacred cup of coffee and read some poetry, meditation, or spiritual guidance book, my heart completely open and unfiltered. I had to do it immediately, before the crushing sadness or depression kicked in and clouded the reception, expertly engaging my filters and defenses. I knew the porousness of those early morning moments were essential to learning how to take my next steps, step by step. Slow, slow.

That same spring and summer, my good friends Sharon and Mike returned from a three-week trip in Central Europe. One of the stories I was most captivated by was the story of the city of Budapest which I had not visited since early 1989 immediately before and after the fall of communism and the Berlin Wall. When liberated from the Soviets, Budapest chose not to tear down and destroy the statues commemorating the Soviet era as so many other cities had. Instead, they kept the statues and moved them to a place on the outskirts of town, clustering all of them together in a park, Memorial Park. It was their visual vow to each other, their country, and the world, to never forget the horrors and the terrors of those awful years, and to keep the memory present in their lives. I was struck by the courage and long view to do that. After hearing about this park I wanted to move forward, with resilience, towards healing, not in a single "bounce" but gradually staying in the aperture of openness and growth. Grief and resilience are a mobius strip for me, a single sided strip having only one edge that becomes a two-dimensional object. It's a paradox, reflected by Rumi:

> *The Way of Love is not a subtle argument:*
> *The door there is devastation.*
> *Birds make great circles of their*
> *freedom. How do they learn it?*
> *They fall, and by falling, they are given wings.*

So that was the answer. Grief and resilience are possible not by a single bounce, or just "getting over it and moving on," but circling and falling, and knowing my wings will catch me when it's time. That's faith. That's resilience. Funny. Nowhere does Rumi talk about grit.

I learned I became a Radical Receiver when I had no choice or other option. When my system of body, heart, brain, and spirit went into shock, they all stood still. Usual autonomic reflexes of fight or flight were not available, so I learned through my own first-hand experience, there is a third option: stand still – not in fear or paralysis - but in openness, love.

My body and brain shut down at the moment of convergence of two unthinkable events, each on its own unimaginable and together unspeakably unimaginable. I could not rationally grasp onto anything with my body and heart in consuming grief. I could not make any decisions through the relentless pain. I was just open, porous, and permeable. It was in those moments that love began flowing into me through sources around me who love and care for me. I had no power or energy to resist, defend, feel guilt at or resistance to accepting help. I could only, in that moment, say "Yes" to receiving the acts of unfiltered love and caring that were washing my way.

I am known for being strong and competent, just like my friend at the beach café said. I am known for my Texas Grit. Everyone reminded me of it the day my mother died, and my marriage unilaterally ended. My strength usually looks like fierce independence. "No thank you. I can handle that." "Thanks for the offer, but I don't want to inconvenience you." "Yes, I've got a plan all worked out and here's what it is." "Thanks, but (fill in the blank)." When I became immobilized with pain and grief I found I was only capable of saying, "Yes, thank you." "Yes, I will accept your offer of shelter, safe harbor, and hospitality." "Yes, thank you. I would like to meet you for lunch/tea/coffee/wine and talk with you." "Yes, thank you. I will (fill in the blank.)" I felt a depth of new freedom by absorbing, receiving, and letting these beautiful gifts wash over and through me. No strings attached. No need to defend or feel the need to reciprocate. I was simply receiving in a radical way – a new and transformative experience for me. The aperture was turned wide, the view broadened, the light poured in, and I could begin to see possibilities far out in the distance that weren't observable when I focused only on my loss, my pain.

If Radical Receiving on my part requires nothing more than being still, keeping my heart undefended and simply letting love and concern and support wash over me and into me, then, please, tell me what is so radical about it? Maybe because we are bio-evolutionarily programmed against it?

What I wasn't taught but have learned when I look back on those days of The Great Shit Storm, is that it is radical because my being still and open and receiving is a deep and powerful gift to the giver. It allows those who love me to find an open channel to give that love and have it received 100%—no defenses, no judgements, no expectations for the tedious exchange called "reciprocity." It goes against my own family's insistence we be beholden to no one, because therein lies vulnerability, and that very vulnerability is the enemy, or so I was taught.

One of the few pieces of advice my mother gave me was shared with me when I left Hyphen-Husband (#2). All she said was "Never let him know he got to you." Now I choose a different path. My porousness allows the giver to give unconditionally, lovingly, in ways that they alone can uniquely give to me, and they are richer for it. It allows them to do something other than stand helplessly by and witness my pain. Resilience, then, is not the priority. I can see now that working on resilience and recovery comes more genuinely, and I am more ready for it, if I can be still and receive. What if I were able to do that gracefully on a regular basis using just the currency of openness, acceptance, and love? It would require my continued presence in the present and remembering the true currency exchange. I wondered at the time if I would be able to stand still like the hummingbird, slowly moving through each day, which leads into each tomorrow, and so on. So the trick was not "picking myself up and dusting myself off" after all.

There is a paradox of getting stronger by allowing more vulnerability. It has not been lost on me. I have gotten stronger by allowing my Texas roots, some formed generations ago when the Georgia cotton farmer Dempsey Abiah Morgan moved from Long Cane, Georgia to Brenham, Texas in 1832 to grow cotton and raise his family – literally putting down new physical roots in Texas. New roots also went down and grew deep over the years with the friends I made here: the girlfriends I made in high school that are still friends today; boys I dated who introduced me to the rivers of San Antonio and the Hill Country, jalapeno peppers, and their stories of cattle rancher and oil men ancestors; my cotton-farmer-daddy sorority sisters; my summer church camps in the appropriately named little town of Comfort.

Unknowingly, the roots grew deeper every spring with the riotous outbursts of bluebonnets and Indian blankets, flowing springs and ancient wells and deep blue, cold, natural swimming holes. All those years in New York and Connecticut and New England those roots were here in the Texas Hill Country, growing deep, growing strong, waiting for me to return when I needed them most, as they knew I would.

All the Roots Grow Deeper When It's Dry

Lyrics and Music by David Wilcox

Summer lasted a generation
A generation – and then the winter wind
The bounty harvest that seemed so endless
It seemed so endless until it gave what it could give

Prosperity will have its seasons
Even when it's here, it's going by
And when it's gone, we pretend to know the reason
All the roots grow deeper when it's dry.

It looked so easy, we change the weather
We would turn this world ourselves, this world so small
But slower rhythms - still unheard of
Said that every blessed summer someday had to fall.

Prosperity will have its seasons
Even when it's here, it's going by
And when it's gone, we pretend to know the reason
All the roots grow deeper when it's dry, when it's dry

7 – THE PITFALLS AND PERILS OF A HAPPY CHILDHOOD

A happy childhood… is the worst preparation for life.

~ Kinky Friedman
American singer, songwriter, humorist,
and former candidate for Governor of Texas

The problem with having a happy childhood is I assumed it would always be that way. So how did I get to Texas again after forty three years, heading into my third divorce?

My first experience of Texas Culture Shock hit me with a smack up the side of my unfashionably curly-haired teenage head when I returned to Texas the first time at the age of fourteen after a brief detour in Washington, D.C., where Daddy had been stationed. I left a pre-teen /early teen, urban/suburban culture, Bass Weejuns wearing (without socks of course and, for God's sake, without pennies), with super cool Madras Bermuda shorts, Peter Pan collared blouses, and nylon "baggies" made famous and de rigueur by the Beach Boys' "Surfin' USA" in the early 60s. I'd been dancing at eighth grade school dances and seventh and eighth grade recreation room parties for just as long, and yes, the slow-dancing-snuggled-up-too-close slow dances where small, fledgling erections could be felt against my leg as we danced, both of us pretending not to notice.

I landed that summer in the church youth group of Trinity Baptist Church in San Antonio, admittedly, in hindsight, a liberal church, certainly by today's (and the rest of Texas') standards. The teenage girls still wore white bobby socks and white tennis shoes, unbelievably enough, together. It was a world where I was initiated into the civil rights movement with sermons about freedom and equality, singing "We Shall Overcome" at Sunday night youth campfires, along with the faintly sinful "Mountain Dew." We sang "Kumbaya," often with the accompanying sign language and none of the irony with which the song and phrase would come to be inextricably linked. This world lived side by side in a world where a particularly pious high school freshman-to-be whispered in judgmental tones that *she* did not dance and didn't approve of those who did because "too often a prom gown was exchanged for a maternity dress." This of course barely crossed my mind over the next few years while I was flailing The Monkey or The Watusi or The Mashed Potato and especially during those too-close slow dances. But I wanted to fit in, and I was always good at fitting in. I cut back on the dances and didn't talk about them at all when I was at church.

I recall that summer of my first transition back to Texas before freshman year of high school as a sweet and easy time. When days begin to turn the Texas Hill Country's version of autumn, they become even sweeter. Days stay warm into the late fall, but the light shifts suddenly and becomes pure gold in the mornings, bathing every leaf of the massive live oaks with dark copper shimmering glory. The days, while pleasantly warm, eventually relent to chilled evenings, perfect for light sweaters at the ubiquitous football games or campfires with S'mores. Seriously. S'mores. Made the old-fashioned messy way. As I write this decades later my Inner Skeptic insists that my life could not have been so idyllic - friends with similar, positive, supportive values; parents in intact loving families who loved us and supported us but never hovered. I had a wonderful boy-friend from my church group by that time, and separate, but equally wonderful, high school friends and experiences. Of course as an adult I wonder in hindsight who knew what was actually going on in those marriages and homes?

If I were reading this in anyone else's memoir I'd declare, "What clueless solipsistic bullshit!" (or something like that.) At the very least I would accuse the writer of succumbing to the chief danger of memoir, one that is all but inevitable – selective memory or reconstructing memories. We all do it. But writers write it down for ourselves and others to hold up to the lights of time and scrutiny, so it needs to be true to the best of our ability. At my fiftieth high school reunion I learned the different truth of some of my classmates; angry fathers returning from wars we barely knew about to homes they barely remembered; secret pregnancies conveniently shuttled off to other parts of the world under plausible stories of routine transfers; an unbearable home life buried in the mane of a beloved horse at the post stable, ridden hard every day until the wind and time dried tears; cracks in the seeming racial equality in our tight world, racism simmering but optically contained with tight military structure.

In my world none of these things existed because I didn't see them. They didn't exist or were dead to me, just like Schrodinger's Cat.[10] My observation made it so. It's one of the reasons remembering, reflection, and recollection of events seem to shift over years. We are the observer but are always changing and shifting ourselves. What usually remains are emotions and feelings associated with an event which come through, in hindsight, as truth. A sound that triggers a gut response of fear and the flash of being afraid in a dark cellar but we can't remember why. A song that brings us back to a time at Christmas singing with the family, the taste of gingerbread still on your tongue, recalling a place, a person. A scent that reminds you of the inside of your grandmother's purse.

The Irish philosopher and poet, John O'Donohue stated in his book *Walking in Wonder:*

> *There is a place where our vanished days secretly gather. Memory, as a kingdom, is full of the ruins of presence…Sometimes the needle of thought finds its way into a groove of memory and suddenly an old experience that you no longer remembered comes back almost pure and fresh and intact to you.*

Why would I ever worry or expect my life, so on track, would ever be otherwise? I didn't. Why would I even be curious about finding other kinds of friends? I wasn't. At the time.

I lived on or around Army posts almost my whole life. Everything about that life felt comfortable, familiar, safe. I rode my bike alone back and forth to school as a seven year-old.

My mother and I often took excursions, just the two us, driving to New Braunfels, about twenty miles north of San Antonio, to the wonderful fabric store there, Comal Cottons, looking at patterns and choosing fabric which then magically turned into summer shorts and tops and dirndl skirts, impressive and complicated Halloween costumes, pajama and robe sets made of soft flannel angel prints, and later, very special occasion party dresses. There was the bubblegum-hot-pink taffeta with a deep V-backed full skirted number I wore to the eighth grade Christmas dance as Mike Toy's date; the deep teal blue velveteen bodice and matching teal taffeta full skirted dress I wore to my going away party at the end of eighth grade, romantically dancing the (early) night away to Bobby Vinton's "Blue Velvet," with my boyfriend, Jimmy Fassbender. Mom also made my GA Queen's white pique floor-length dress with a deep cowl collar. If I still had that dress today, I would wear it. That's how much I loved it. Looking back, I realize how many deep shawl and cowl-collared sweaters and sparkly dress-occasion things I've worn over the years. In a clear act of foreshadowing, the third-grade white taffeta Jayne Mansfieldesque showgirl dress was the first of many similar, elegant gowns I would wear on the stages of New York cabaret clubs. The Jayne Mansfield dress gave me the same thrill at eight years old I would come to know every time I stepped on a stage and into the spotlight. I'm not sure that's what Jesus had in mind, but I loved it. I think Jesus might have loved it on me as well once he could see and feel my unfettered joy, as the Jesus I knew at that age was totally into joy. Fifty years later I recognize my pre-teen years were swathed in pique, taffeta, velveteen, and Comal cotton, all the loving results of my terribly underappreciated, especially by me, mother.

We were *all* new kids to the school that first year at the new Robert G. Cole Junior-Senior High School, a familiar situation for us for most of our lives. The "New Kid Syndrome" was not as pronounced for us at Cole. We were used to kids coming and going, making new friends then leaving them behind, or being left behind. Early on a friend's mother told me, amidst my tears of leaving my friend, "Honey, there are just as many good friends waiting for you where you're going as you are leaving behind." I must admit, she was right. That would become true of husbands at some point in my life as well and may be why it even felt a little familiar to plug and play. One more loss. On to the next.

Anita, the girl who sat behind me in home room on that first day of school became my best friend through all four years of high school and remains a friend almost six decades later. She had arrived from Orleans, France, where her father had been stationed, a few weeks before school started. She'd been a member of the eighth-grade cheering squad which already gave her points in my book. Hearing stories about her Junior High Prom in some French castle didn't strike me as particularly noteworthy but watching her demonstrate a very different style of cheering from the movements the girls here in the U.S. had studied so closely left us a little puzzled, as if we were watching another language instead of listening to it, although in her case there was some of that, too. Before long we had added her "Hey, Hey, C'est ca c'est? Time to fight and win the day!" along with the soft-rounded arm motions instead of the angular arm and leg thrusts we were used to and secretly practiced for our inevitable some-day cheerleader tryouts.

Anita was a baton twirler though, and a talented one. She quickly earned her spot as one of the high school band twirlers before going on to become Drum Majorette of the band, a musical ensemble that was never quite worthy of her. As much as I loved my school and could sing the Beach Boys' "Be True to Your School" without irony, our high school band was pretty sorry. They were small and definitely not mighty. Maybe all that moving around as Army brats had an impact on the continuing progress of instrument and music mastery. It was not for trying on the part of the band teacher. He directed the band with an observable air of frustration and a frenetic waving of his baton as if the sheer intensity of his physical effort could wrangle notes and showmanship out of his meager material, getting them to at least march in simple formation and straight line. Alas, no.

But Anita was a cut above. I don't think I saw her ever drop the baton during her special spotlight routines. She could fire-baton twirl which was incredibly impressive. Up, and up and up that fire breathing baton would go into the Texas night sky looking like a shooting star, then floating down safely into her experienced hands. Sometimes she tossed two fire-batons during the same routine. There was one irritatingly not so glamorous requirement for these spectacles, however. As Anita's close friend, and solicited by her, I, as one of the cheerleaders, had to squat down no more than twenty feet from her in the center of the football field with a blanket and a bucket of sand which I ungracefully lugged out, requirements of the Ft. Sam Houston Fire Department, just on the off chance her accuracy in tossing and catching met up with the rare bobble.

There was the bleak year when I was in eighth grade when Daddy was sent to Korea, an "unaccompanied tour." I look back at that hard year and all my mother had to handle with two teenagers and a six year old and marvel that she didn't kill us all. If she had, not a jury in the country would have convicted her, and rightly so. From an adult's perspective I also marvel at how hard it must have been and how much work it took to make our family life feel normal during those absences. Like Christmas. I remember that Christmas with Daddy overseas when I got my two Bobbie Brooks crewneck sweaters, one red, one black, which were exactly what I'd hoped for but didn't want to ratchet up the hope meter too high in anticipation they'd actually appear; my younger brother Ken's cowboy boots, hat, and pistols elicited squeals of delight. Christmas dinner was with my two grandmothers, aunt and uncle and cousins, all of whom lived in the Washington, D.C. area and gave us the rare opportunity of having extended family close by. Did my mother miss my father? I assume so, but she never said so and she never complained to us anyway. "We do what we have to do," she would say.

Wanting "the kids to have a good Christmas" was frequently and poignantly expressed by Daddy, and both Mother and Daddy worked hard at it. Mom always made Mamie

Eisenhower's Million Dollar Fudge, spritz cookies with the cookie gun I never mastered, along with just about anything else found in the kitchen, and later, her famous bourbon balls. I look back now on Christmas morning photos that go back to the early 50's, of the "haul" for my older brother and I and have absolutely no idea how my parents finagled bicycles, chemistry sets, Tiny Tears and Revlon dolls, and, unfortunately, my play kitchen sets and even a play ironing board, a total waste of their money and Santa's time. Not long before Daddy died, I asked him about those Christmases and particularly about the spinet piano they bought for my piano lessons when I was nine. He looked off in the distance for a while as if he were trying to remember himself how they pulled off this astronomical sleight of financial hand, and finally replied, "Six dollars a week for the rest of our lives." I wish I could tell them both how much I appreciate it as an adult. I wish I could tell them a lot of things.

My classmates in the new Texas high school were world travelers, multi-racial, smart, and for the most part, fun. Our school was new and shiny and had the best of everything: language labs, a decent cafeteria, although today I cannot eat or stand the smell of fish sticks which were always on the Friday menu thanks to the Catholic kids. But then, I'd be surprised if even they could stand that smell today either. We had some good and talented teachers and the usually statistically present smattering of losers. We boasted a spectacular football stadium with groomed fields, new stadium seats, and a fully lit field of stadium lights, perfect for all our night games, most of which were played on our home field for obvious reasons. We were in the Friday Night Lights heartland, after all. Other football fields in the small Texas towns we played were often littered with potholes and even the occasional cow patty. I know now our teachers were exceptional almost across the board in no small part due to the fact we were a federal institution and teaching jobs were GS (Government Service) rated jobs and filled by competitive exams, just like any senior federal job.

But we were the fishes in the water and knew no other life. Our school lives and our community lives and our social lives were seamlessly interconnected and held together by the boundaries of the military life and values: serving our country; never bringing disrespect on our fathers because everything reflected on them and their careers; knowing we were different from other families in ways our young lives couldn't necessarily calibrate.

Returning to Texas the second time during The Great Shitstorm, knowing no one other than my brother and sister-in-law in their small Texas town, creating beginnings, scoping out the social scenes and social groups, I began to realize how special my life was growing up. It seemed every parent knew every child and every child knew every parent or at least knew who each child was and, probably more importantly, who their parents were. We knew we could never get away with anything without our parents finding out, like getting a traffic ticket or even a warning on post, "papering" some friend's house in the middle of the night or skipping school. We knew there was always someone, many someones, to rely on. I only heard about these infractions, of course, because I was always safe at home in my own bed after midnight, never venturing out. Good girl stuff.

If I were driving across post or in the car with someone who was and it was 5:00, all traffic stopped. If the driver was an active or retired military person they got out of the car, saluted towards the flag that was being lowered on the main concourse accompanied by the military music of "Retreat." When it finished, traffic started up again. I went to sleep every night to

the sound of "Taps" played by the carillon in the Quadrangle of
Fort Sam Houston, an old stone Army barracks famous for
both housing Geronimo after his capture and housing a flock of
peacocks who currently wandered at will through the Quadrangle. The officers' kids and the enlisted men's kids played
together on the sports teams, papered the houses at night with
their friends, dated each other, and hung out at The Teen Club
on post. In my memory there were no distinctions, but there
probably were some in other kids' minds. We all had dads in
the Army doing their jobs – doctors, dentists, technical jobs,
planning and office jobs, teaching and training troops, and
coming to our football games and school plays if they could.

Our moms were the ones who took up the slack. Today I look
at them as unsung rock stars of stability. They kept the family
operation going with discipline, countless trips to the mall,
sandwiches for the track meets, and every PTA meeting.

On the first day of my junior year of high school I sat next to a
boy I had sat next to in second grade at Fort Sam Houston
Elementary. Today I realize that my parents' experience living
their last years at the Army Residence Community among old
friends and colleagues must have been an amplified version of
that life. Living in a military community instills a powerful sense
of community and belonging that we, as kids, certainly were not
aware of at the time. For us, it was just the way life was. It also
created a sense of unarticulated longing and belonging that I
sometimes felt as an adult out there in the world, sometimes so
busy with life I had few friends, and the friends I had lived all
across the country. Often it felt like there was no center of
gravity for any of it. "Where are you from?" people ask
sometimes. "Where is home?" The only true answer was to
disavow it. The answer was so deeply embedded it could never

be articulated, so the response was "I was raised in the military…" Assumptions took over the rest.

I felt as deeply known, held, and loved in my other world at Trinity Baptist Church and especially the Youth Group that was the epicenter of my world there. Me and High School Boyfriend Bob. First Kiss Bob. First Serious Make Out Boyfriend Bob. His mother taught me to fry fresh-shot quail and make chili rellenos and chicken fried steak on the weekends I traveled with them to the rustic family ranch ninety miles west of San Antonio. High School Boyfriend Bob and I would go quail hunting, well, he hunted, and I tagged along. But he did teach me to clean the craw of the shot quail, scooping out the seed sack from the neck with my index and middle fingers after twisting the head off. The seed made a sound as it hit the rusted corrugated metal wall of the nearby barn that sounded like gentle rainfall on a summer evening. Later, there would be the smell of quail frying up in his mother's ancient cast iron skillet, along with chili rellenos, and, always, pecan pie. Today, chili rellenos and chicken fried steak are about the only original dishes I can make and, I might add, wow my New York friends with the sheer exotic fare. Well, that and King Ranch Chicken. It didn't seem to occur to my own mother to teach me to cook anything. Anything. Odd, in retrospect. And it apparently didn't occur to me to ask her or show any interest. Maybe that's one of the reasons several of the men I have loved, married, or lived with, not always necessarily or successfully in that or any order, are excellent cooks.

I loved High School Boyfriend Bob and together we navigated the wonderful, thrilling, confusing territory of first love and first touch, held in a context of church and church family. We always knew how far was far enough. There was no debate about sex or "how far." It simply was not up for discussion let alone debate. "It" was never going to happen. And it didn't. That purity thing from my early Southern Baptist church and Girls Auxiliary days was firmly locked in place, and I could often hear the clatter of new rubies rubbing together. Nothing since has ever felt so romantically right as navigating our worlds as such a confident young couple. I felt the rightness to my bones and knew that I was living the model life I had set for myself. Stay on the path. Stay the course. Happiness and fulfillment right this way. Christian wife and motherhood straight ahead. I had, after all, already fallen in love "forever."

By the time high school graduation came around I'd added Head Cheerleader, Sophomore Class President, National Honor Society, Junior Play, and yearbook Literary Editor to my burgeoning list of "credentials." This was decades before creating resumes for high schoolers began in Pre-K and was considered an imperative for getting into the so-called Best Colleges, the list of which I couldn't have named because I didn't know there was such a list. Instead of worrying about getting the right summer internship in an environmental non-profit devoted to climate change, or finagling a delegate spot at an international Youth for Peace conference in Norway, my best friend Anita and I got jobs at our local Winn-Dixie Five and Dime where we straightened up the perpetually cluttered bins of sewing notions, nails and screws, put the GI Joes back in their proper boxes when we weren't contorting them into compromising positions, and ate a lot of colorfully printed tin foil covered chocolate footballs located beside the big brass cash register. In spite of that ordinary low-level part-time teenage job I learned one of the greatest management and leadership lessons I would ever learn from Mr. Rickman, our store manager.

It was a couple of days before Christmas and the five and dime
was doing a very brisk business. Wrapping paper, candy canes,
stocking stuffers, stuffed animals and dolls were flying out the
door, along with the popular G.I. Joes. Anita and I had full
schedules of holiday things to do ourselves, of course, including
Christmas Eve with our families and particularly our boyfriends.
I asked Mr. Rickman when we would close the store on
Christmas Eve.

"Well, as soon as we see things are tapering off, we can close.
But as long as there are enough customers, we need to be
open." That evening, after Mr. Rickman left the store, I went to
work. I made a small sign a few inches tall and a few inches
wide on a piece of yellow paper I found by the cash register.
The sign read, "Please help us go home early Christmas Eve.
Remember everything you need now." I taped it by the handle
of the front door where everyone entering the store would
surely see it.

The next afternoon Anita and I arrived after school to work at
the Winn-Dixie as usual. Mr. Rickman greeted us and calmly
said he wanted all of us in his office in the back of the store.
Anita and I hung up our coats and walked back to his office,
past the G.I. Joes and down the aisles with sewing notions and
big pattern books, along with the other two employees, a plump
older lady (or at least she seemed at the time) and Mr. Black, the
tall, scrawny, acned, and much detested assistant manager. I was
nervous but couldn't quite put my finger on why. We crowded
into the office.

"The district manager paid me a surprise visit this morning
doing his usual rounds. Imagine my surprise when he told me
about a note taped on our front door. He was not happy at all.
Now, I don't need or want to know who did it." (There was no

need as Anita's eyes widened as she clapped her hand over her mouth, looked at me, and commenced with her customary fierce blush all the way to her hairline.) "However, we need to agree that those kinds of things are not very professional and are an example of things we need to talk about either privately with me or together as a group of employees. So, I'm just asking you not to do something like that again without talking it over with me first."

The minute he'd started talking I knew what it was going to be about. My face burned with shame and embarrassment and my heart pounded beneath my Bobbie Brooks red crew neck sweater. I hurried out of the room with the others. I knew of course, I'd have to tell him it was me. I figured he'd fire me, and rightly so, but how was I ever going to tell my parents or live this down? I walked back to his office and shut the door and confessed the deed. He said, "I know it was you, Chickie, but there was no need to single you out. I tell you what…I'll stay as late as anyone and everyone on Christmas Eve and maybe together we can all get out of here early and enjoy our time with family and friends. How does that sound?" Well, it sounded great. Really great. Mr. Rickman was my first boss and would always be one of the two best bosses I ever had over the next sixty years.

Fifty years later, visiting my parents in San Antonio and my brother and sister-in-law over Christmas, I struck up a conversation over cookies and hot chocolate with my brother's next-door neighbor. We were making small talk about my visit and my growing up in San Antonio, and it prompted me to tell him about my job at Winn-Dixie and the Christmas when I pulled the stunt with the note on the front door. Next Door Neighbor Mike said, "One of my earliest jobs out of college was working for Winn-Dixie in San Antonio. I remember that store."

"Well, my boss, Mr. Rickman, taught me a lot that Christmas and I've always been grateful."

"Did you say his name was Mr. Rickman? *I* worked for Mr. Rickman and he was the best boss *I* ever had!" And then we were off on a two-person Mr. Rickman Story Fest. It was many years later while working with a Fortune 500 corporation in New York I heard the summary of Mr. Rickman's management philosophy spoken by arguably one of the most famous CEOs of the decade: "Fix the problem, not the blame." I learned it at sixteen. I thought that was how the work world worked. Another pitfall on my way to adulthood. Unfortunately, I was wrong.

During those San Antonio Texas Hill Country days my friends and I would spend long summer days floating in big black inner tubes with groups of friends down the languid rivers threading the rolling Texas Hill Country, one of its many secret treasures. Emphasis on secret, so even though I've shared with you, please don't take it any further. Those tubes bore no re-semblance to the mega "Toobing" industry which attracts thousands of kids today lashed together as huge beer drinking amoeba-like flotillas, never venturing the rapids or anything else for that matter.

For one week out of the summer we would attend our high school youth group church camp in Comfort, Texas—a tiny town about forty miles north of San Antonio. Trinity Baptist Church had its own church ranch on 200 acres of hilltop with boys' and girls' dormitories, a dining hall, an open-air stone chapel and large swimming pool where separate swim times for boys and girls were closely monitored. The evenings were for "fellowship" time, and at the end of the week, the big entertainment production was a group of us campers, fully costumed, presenting "Who Rustled Them Thar White-Faced Cattle off the Wide-Open Texas Range." It was written as a melodrama with the starring roles played by High School Boy Friend Bob and me, naturally. It was a clever production and in the end the cowboy gets a pie in the face - and the girl. On our two-week Trinity Baptist Youth Choir tour to the west coast the following summer, we presented it in church fellowship halls after our church concerts in sanctuaries, to great amusement and acclaim where the cowboy (High School Boyfriend Bob) still always got the girl (me). Cue big hug and kiss. Always a crowd pleaser. It's funny how much of the actual script I remember. I also remember the summer production of "OklaHamlet," a musical production for summer camp with show stopping numbers such as "People Will Say We're Insane," and "Blood Is Gushing Out All Over" ("all over the throne room and the floor. Hemoglobin is a creeping and the blood it is a seeping all around room and even out the door….") There was no end of creative and musically creative talent to write and produce these things.

I met soon-to-be West Point Starter Husband, a boy from Lubbock, Texas, who was at the U.S. Military Academy, through a classmate of his who was going through Jungle Training School in Panama. It was a very big deal for me being in Panama for Texas Tech summer breaks and holidays while Daddy was stationed there. It was, quite simply, Nirvana for a college co-ed. Panama is the only place in the world where all four major types of jungle grow, and at the height of the Vietnam War, the Jungle Training School ensured that cadets from military academies around the world flocked there for the two week jungle training course. Those weeks looked like this for me and all the other "young ladies" on the Pacific side of the Canal Zone:

On Saturday morning, multiple plane loads of cadets from various corners of the world would descend, literally, in the Canal Zone. The Commander of Ft. Amador felt obligated, in the best sense, to entertain the "young ladies" in the Canal Zone on the various posts, and hosted a formal dance where cadets and ladies would mix and mingle and do what young cadets and young ladies do – conveniently fall in love and have the benefit of a young dashing escort, or for the cadets, officers' daughters around the isthmus at the numerous events and activities, beach parties and home cooked meals, dinners at the Officers' Club, moonlight beach picnics, as well as private rendezvous, where Francois, or Santiago, or Charles, or Bentley would squire their companions. Ceviche ran rampant and Cuba Libres flowed freely. Two weeks later on Saturday, I, er, I mean the young ladies, would be back at the airport, on the tarmac, tearfully waving goodbye with a white hankey to Francois, Santiago, Charles, or Bentley as the wheels of the plane lifted off the runway – with just enough time to rush home and dress for the Saturday night ball where I, uh, we, could meet John, or Peter, or Jules, or…well you get the picture. This went on all summer long.

As I've aged, I reflect more on the little hinges of serendipity, some call it fate, some call it divine guidance or a Godwink, some call it luck, that our lives and paths and choices reflectively bounce off of. If I had been standing at the punch bowl at the table on the other side of that ballroom in Panama instead of where I was, I wouldn't have met the gentleman who knew the young man from Lubbock—who I later gave my name and number to. The Boy from God's Left Elbow did call, but he was always in upstate New York at The Academy when I was in school in Lubbock. I was always in Panama when he was back home for the holidays. I honestly don't remember how we got together for any first date, but we must have.

Two and a half years later we were standing at the altar in the chapel at Trinity Baptist Church – a chapel named after the deceased father of High School Boy Friend Bob, an irony not lost on me. And there it was, in the stroke of a single "I Do," I segued from Happy Childhood to Prospects. Security. Love forever. Couldn't have been simpler. Life was easy and the world was safe. The only problem was it didn't feel like that with the exceptions of the Prospects and the Security. There wasn't much sizzle, just acknowledgement that we'd "married well." I would continue in my mother's footsteps. I described it as "a marriage made in the Pentagon if not heaven." It started as a joke but came true too soon.

Blanco River Meditation #2

Music and Lyrics by Walt Wilkins and Kent Finlay

I got no line, I got no pole
I just brought time to this old fishing hole
The sky is blue, the water's clear
I got all I need right here
A little shade, a little sun
I've got nothing to do
And I'm not leaving till I'm done

There's a blue cat on the bottom
And a bullfrog on the bank
I just pitched a pretty pebble
And watched the ripples while it sank
Hear the crickets in the meadow
Sing the song they've always sung
I've got nothing to do all day
And I'm not leaving till I'm done

Well, I'm not leaving till I'm done
I'm not leaving till I'm through
Slowing down this crazy life
For just a day or two
Yeah, and think I'll hang right here
And watch the river run
I've got nothing to do,
And I'm not leaving till I'm done.

8 – What Ifs and If Onlys

If ifs and buts were candy and nuts, we'd all have a Merry Christmas.

~ Don Meredith, Dallas Cowboys Quarterback
Sports Commentator, Actor

I bet we all do it, this game of "What If?" What if I'd done this rather than that? What if I'd taken that other job? What if I'd gone with this person? I know you do, too, because I've had some of these conversations with you. After the shock of The Great Shitstorm and all the time I had on my travels for those months, I think a lot about what might have been different. I was on one path and clearly ended up on another, not necessarily a bad one, but definitely different. There were some dark nights of the soul where I just wanted to blame West Texas for my ending up on some different paths, although I know it's not fair. Okay. Maybe a little fair. But the bigger question remains: How did I get from where I thought I'd be to where I've ended up?

In the years before I went to college at Texas Tech University, I occasionally allowed myself to think, when I really thought about college at all, about Trinity University in San Antonio. It is a small, beautiful, red brick liberal arts college on a hill, shaded by large long-limbed oak trees overlooking the city from its skyline campus. There is a carillon that rings out over the campus from the tall tower that is now its iconic symbol, and a beautiful fountain. Every time I'd been on the campus for one reason or another I'd felt at home, but I always knew it was out of reach, aspirationally as well as financially. My soul belonged there, but my background and upbringing could never get me there. The closest I came to belonging is immortalized in a black and white photograph on the last page of my senior high school yearbook, a silhouette at the fountain, holding hands (for photographic purposes only, allegedly) with a boy who has become a fine man and to this day a gentle and sweet friend.

Neither of my parents graduated from traditional college and my brother and I were the first ones in our family to go. I went to an excellent high school and still had zero college counseling. My parents were not able to provide much guidance in that area. My excellent high school provided no guidance either to help me understand how scholarships worked or how to attain one. No one in my family, including, if not especially, me, thought to ask because a state school was always in the plans, if any of us had ever thought to really make any plans, which we didn't. My grades were good. I probably could have qualified back then. It wasn't until years later I ever considered that a college should be chosen for what it could provide academically and how it could prepare me as an adult. I thought it was just another check mark on the way to my married life. I always knew I would graduate. It would help me be that "asset" to my future husband, as I was repeatedly reminded. What if I had gone to Trinity University and never met the cowboys and cotton farmers, and their daughters and girlfriends? What if I'd become the writer I knew I was and could be? Maybe. I was on the trajectory to marry High School Boyfriend Bob anyway so it made sense to follow him to Lubbock. What if I'd never had to spend my college years gritting my teeth against the West Texas dust storms walking to class?

It was also the mid-sixties and I had not been exposed to anything like the women's movement or feminism. Little of that progressive thinking had taken root in the culture of conserveative middle America, let alone in my all-American military family. Betty Friedan's *The Feminine Mystique*, Marilyn French's *The Women's Room*, and Erica Jong's *Fear of Flying*, all of which would become hard core staples in the canon of my new life, had not yet come crashing onto my cultural scene. It was a little too early for that. The National Organization for Women was founded in June of 1966, the summer I was blissfully enjoying Padre Island Beach between my junior and senior years of high school, going to beach parties and Trinity Baptist Church Youth Camp in Comfort, Texas. I had heard about some kind of birth control pill, but what did that have to do with me if I were saving myself for marriage? What if I'd gotten that pill somehow? What if I'd felt free to use it?

At home my senior year I was watching *The Carol Burnett Show*, *The Andy Griffith Show* and of course, *The Ed Sullivan Show*, where a few years earlier I had gawked at the Beatles as well as a short-haired clean-shaven newcomer named Willy Nelson wearing a charcoal suit, white shirt, and necktie singing "Ghost Riders in the Sky." I danced to music at the Teen Club on Fort Sam Houston and at High School Boyfriend Bob's Senior Parties given by his classmates at tony Alamo Heights High School at tony venues around the city. "California Dreaming" and other Mamas and Papas hits, "96 Tears," "Strangers in the Night," "Cherish" by the Association, and, of course, anything by The Righteous Brothers populated my high school soundtrack. Lush extravaganzas like *Dr. Zhivago*, *The Sound of Music*, and even the improbable Charlton Heston in *The Ten Commandments* played in the movie theaters. On the fringes of these bouncy, upbeat, schmaltzy tunes and wholesome upbeat television shows, the early shadows of the growing, darkening (in my family's eyes) culture change began to appear on *The Smothers Brothers Show*, the popular song "The Ballad of the Green Beret," or in Otis Redding's "When a Man Loves a Woman," which made me ache for something I had no idea how to define. There were the

sexually charged lyrics from The Rolling Stones, and Bob
Dylan's stream of consciousness. Lyndon Johnson was
President because of "that terrible business in Dallas" back in
1963, and there was background noise on the family television
about some place called Vietnam, wherever that was, and a war
someplace far away. It didn't concern me much. During those
high school years in the early 1960s I began to hear about some
classmates whose fathers had been killed in Vietnam. I was only
barely aware of it because of Huntley and Brinkley on the
Nightly News. For a military kid living on an Army post, it was
all oddly remote.

San Antonio was and still is a world apart from the High Plains
of West Texas, as that elevated, bone dry part of Texas is
known. San Antonio was a decent sized city with the McNay
Art Institute, museums, even a famous French restaurant, La
Louisiane, a "special place" restaurant, although paradoxically
founded and owned for several generations by a Greek family. I
recall eating there only one time because my parents considered
it too expensive, too pretentious, and "not the kind of food we
eat." La Louisiane sits in the pantheon of familiar and well-
loved restaurants in San Antonio along with the famous Barn
Door Steakhouse which had been there forever, and the 24-
hour Earl Abel's Restaurant which was a faithful supporter and
enabler of many late date nights with its familiar semi-circle red
"leather" banquets. There was the city's Fiesta Celebration in
April every year, including The Battle of Flowers daytime
parades in which our high school band and cheerleaders
marched, sweating profusely and embarrassingly in our long
sleeve high necked velveteen cheerleading uniforms. Those
uniforms were the envy of every cheerleader in every other
school in our district of small, rural, unsophisticated Texas
towns and could proudly stand up in wardrobe style and variety
to the bigger city schools. The San Antonio River nighttime

Flambeau parade, my favorite, flowed through the city on beautifully decorated flower barges lit up with hundreds of torches on the San Antonio River. *Night In Old San Antonio,* was a raucous party of Fiesta bands and art walks and thousands of people cracking confetti filled eggs over the heads of friends and strangers.

The whole event was concocted in 1891 to celebrate the Battle of San Jacinto, the eighteen-minute battle led by Sam Houston that defeated General Santa Anna and the Mexican army to gain Texas' independence, not to be confused with The Battle of the Alamo, although that's probably the only battle in Texas most people recognize. Like most war tales of heroic and thrilling deeds, time has celebrated, or in some cases eradicated, a darkly tinged story with the carefully curated telling. If you like the story of The Alamo and Jim Bowie and Davy Crockett, and the heroics as it is, glorified in museums and History of Texas textbooks, please don't dig too deeply, or take a scholarly look. You'll be disappointed. If you live in Texas today, you won't be able to attend a book reading by Bryan Borrough and Chris Tomlinson, Texas historians and authors of *Forget the Alamo: The Rise and Fall of an American Myth.* Our current governor made sure the event was banned from the University of Texas Bullock Museum for maligning our great heroes.

The magnificent downtown Majestic and Aztec Theaters in San Antonio were cavernous, created to resemble faux Mexican towns or entire landscapes, topped off, literally, with sky filled constellations of stars. High School Boyfriend Bob and I saw all the big screen movies of the 1960s there. Years later, when my parents moved into their independent living complex in San Antonio, they insisted I look through my psychedelic orange and pink 1960s zippered cloth and plastic suitcase moldering in their attic for forty-five years or have everything in it tossed out that day in the trash. The garish suitcase was the central depository of my precious high school keepsakes and treasures. There I found the movie theater ticket stubs for *The Sound of Music* from Christmas Day 1965. The movie ticket itself was a work of art with the graphic of Julie Andrews twirling against the Alps imprinted on it.

I had no way of thinking about how important the cultural environment could be to me in moving from San Antonio to Lubbock. My home, such as it was in any military family, was in the Panama Canal Zone, or Germany, or Washington, D.C., or San Antonio. I was used to packing up and moving and leaving one locale for another. I never gave any thought about where I was heading because it simply was not in the equation to do so. Resisting or complaining was not an option. The familiar family admonition was offered again: "Honey, you have two choices. You can adjust or you can adjust." I remember receiving the news about upcoming moves with a frisson of anticipation. I'm sure this family-rooted but geographically peripatetic life as a child is why I was so flexible after I went out on my own as an adult. Maybe. Maybe not.

I was not prepared for the huge alien backwater of West Texas. For the 25,000 students who didn't live within 100 miles of the campus and attended Texas Tech as their cowboy or agricultural birthright, pledging their mother's sorority or their father's fraternity along the way, sometimes more than 800 miles from their home, it was a mecca known for being "the farthest I could get away from home and still go to a state school." There's an academic endorsement. I couldn't go to Trinity University because we couldn't afford it. Period. The difference between $25 per credit hour at Trinity, and $50 total for eighteen credit hours at a state school made any conversation irrelevant, especially with parents who were in awe of their children going to any college anywhere, a privilege they had never been afforded or had the opportunity until much later in life to take advantage of. My parents had warned me I might have to spend my first two years at Balboa Community College in the Canal Zone. Shoot me first. There were plenty of guns around everywhere. It would have been easy. The rolling tumbleweeds of West Texas were a welcome runner up. In reflection, I've come to believe there was a greater opportunity cost over a lifetime that surpassed any additional tuition required of attending a university that may have encouraged my intellectual capacities and pursuits and not just my participation as a Miss Lubbock finalist. What if I had found a way or was encouraged to attend Trinity?

Many years later, I began working in New York City in one of the premier corporate divisions of Chase Manhattan Bank at One Chase Plaza in downtown lower Manhattan, the flagship office building. One Chase Plaza was erected in the 1960s, the first significant building built since the depression of the 1930s. It was the first International Style building in lower Manhattan and was created with a large public plaza. I was thrilled walking across the plaza looking up for the first time at Jean Dubuffet's forty foot tall "Group of Four Trees" sculpture commissioned by David Rockefeller. All around me people spoke of that sculpture with awe. I had no idea who Jean Dubuffet was. Four years earlier I'd been back in dusty Lubbock working out a divorce agreement with Starter Husband. Now I was in New York City working with bankers from New York University, Barnard College, Radcliff, Cornell University, Boston College, and even a Yalie or two. I began to understand that *going* to college was not the same as going to *just any* college. It mattered *where* you'd gone – at least here. Instinctively I knew talking about Texas Tech University was not going to do me any favors climbing the corporate ladder. I just shut up. The only way I revealed my educational legacy, usually when asked in social situations, was to make a joke about it. I don't even remember all the jokes I made, but I'm quick and good at those things so I played The Texas Card in a self-deprecating way whenever possible.

I picked up the dress code in the corporate world quickly. As a military kid I'd learned to suss out any new situation quickly, especially fashion requirements, since they are an important part of military life, as well as different styles and cultures at the schools I attended, skills that have served me well over a lifetime.

I quickly discerned the protocols for the Officers' Dining Rooms in both One Chase Plaza and One New York Plaza a few blocks south, but the feeling of being an Outsider always lurked. I was thrust into the rarefied atmosphere of the world of David Rockefeller. It *was* his world – literally. One day, waiting in line to be seated in the Officers Dining Room at One Chase Plaza, I casually leaned against a small painting on the wall by the reception podium. My boss Stan leaned over and said, "You might not want to do that. It's a Picasso." Rockefeller's world was informed and accented by art everywhere. When people were promoted to Vice President, in addition to a significant increase in signing authority on behalf of the corporation and admittance into the first class corporate gym, one of the rituals was to pick out art for your office. My first office, on the 27th floor of New York Plaza, had a panoramic view of Governors Island. Limos to Grand Central Station and Penn Station were mandatory after 6:00 because it wasn't "safe" to take the sub-way from lower Manhattan. That was okay with me.

I had a travel budget I was never quite able to spend. Returning from New Orleans after my first real business trip for the bank, my boss Stan called to me as I walked on the quiet carpet in the hallway by his office. "I need to see you about your trip expenses." This is it, I thought. I've been found out. He knows I'm a fraud, I spent too much money because I didn't know how to act, and I'll be fired. "I send you on these trips to meet people, build relationships, and network," he said. "You didn't spend nearly enough money to let me know you accomplished that." A lesson I never had to be taught again.

It wasn't the classic imposter syndrome, exactly, more like a chronic edgy awareness that I was different, lesser. I always felt I was batting out of my league, but I am good at blending in, acting "as if." In hindsight I guess my smarts, my ability to engage people of different backgrounds, and my focused ambition opened doors in a time that would be much more difficult today. I did miss a cue or two, however, in the vastly multicultural world I was now moving in. Stan, a true mentor and good friend for all the years we worked together, and since, once commented as we walked through the buffet line at One New York Plaza, "Every time you order pastrami on white bread with mayo, somewhere in the world a Jew dies." Once I was out of Texas my education came quickly and fiercely.

All of that education came after my dust-infused West Texas days. The beginning of my sophomore year at Texas Tech had rolled around and I was tired of the whole West Texas thing. High School Boyfriend Bob and I broke up after a four-year dating life together. I wanted to know what else was out there, especially beyond the flat, almost treeless prairie of the High Plains of the Texas Panhandle, cowgirls, and ag students. I also wanted to know who was out there in terms of boys who were not necessarily "good young men," proper, strong, riddled with integrity, usually churchgoing. At the time, of course, I had no idea how rare such beings are, the unicorns of the dating world, and I had one, a rare starfish I wanted to throw back into the sea. Arrogance. Ignorance. Maybe just naivete. Maybe an innate, undefined, unexpressed yearning or longing. For what? I couldn't have told you.

I called my parents in Panama to tell them I wanted to transfer to The University of Texas in Austin, as far away as I could get from this cowboy-loaded western wasteland where dust storms left mud on my teeth as I walked to class across the huge land grant campus, the non-stop high-plains wind leaving both me and the few trees on the barren landscape at perpetual right angles as we persevered against them. Prairie dogs were no longer a novelty. I'd had enough Missions Nights at the Texas Tech Baptist Student Union. But Daddy, as head of operations and logistics in the Canal Zone, was in the middle of managing yet another Central American coup in Panama, phone lines were all down or busy, and after three days of not being able to get through, and classes and football games soon starting, I gave up and stayed. What if I had gotten a phone line through to my parents that week and moved to Austin?

I met Totally Inappropriate Bad Boy Boyfriend at Glorieta before that sophomore year and life got more interesting. Much more interesting. The Totally Inappropriate Bad Boy Boyfriend I'd been nervous and eager to meet someday had arrived. Someday was finally here.

Up until then I'd been satisfied with meeting the good girl expectations of my parents, teachers, and church leaders. I was, in a word, exemplary. I got good grades. My short skirts were fashionably short but not shockingly so. I still went to church on Sundays. I was ready to break out. Always a late bloomer, I should have done some of this rebelling in high school, but I was too busy with cheerleading, church camp, and sweet dating.

While I was at Texas Tech the world was racing by, changing in dramatic ways that were at odds with the values I was raised with.

Reports of Detroit race riots were growing in the news daily. The Summer of Love was in full bloom in San Francisco. The closest I came to the San Francisco counter-cultural phenomenon was my high school classmate's uncle who allegedly penned the song "If You're Going to San Francisco" – you know, "be sure to wear a flower in your hair…" Martin Luther King Jr. was assassinated. I was in a Baptist Student Union based singing group in my sophomore year – The Las Sonrisas Singers ("The Smiling Ones") consisting of a stand-up bass, two guitars, my current best friend and me as vocalists.
We had spent an evening as the featured entertainment at a Baptist Church supper somewhere outside Fort Worth and were driving back when the bass player said, "Wait! What? Pull over! Quick!" Dr. Martin Luther King Jr. was dead. We turned up the radio as we sat in silence on the side of the road. Assassinated. It was 1968, the year of the Tet Offensive, the year when Vietnam snagged everyone's awareness. Robert F. Kennedy was assassinated. Richard Nixon was elected. The Stonewall Riots occurred in New York City. Woodstock. Families and their draft age sons became loudly divisive about the upcoming draft lottery.

What if I had tried to learn about and understand what was happening instead of being fearful of it and shutting down? What if I had decided to become a part of it?

I walked around the campus trying to reconcile my military and church upbringing with the growing sit-ins and protests on campus. Even on a state school campus in God's Left Elbow, (a disparaging term my mother used to designate something geographically remote and uncultured) Texas, the tension was palpable. My sophomore year, 1968, I pledged a sorority. One miserable night on my way to the weekly meeting at our just-off-campus Lodge, I had to walk through the center of campus where a large sit-in candlelight vigil was being held protesting the Vietnam war. I was wearing my (almost) micro-mini skirt of course, as pants were not yet allowed in the sorority house or anywhere else, and much to my embarrassment, my head was wrapped in a very large ugly head scarf – not a trendy turban or anything so chic as that, but a regular large polyester square headscarf tied tightly under my chin as instructed. I felt ridiculous in the get up, devised by the current members, or "Actives," of the sorority for its embarrassing effect on the Pledge Class. Apparently, we Pledges had "disrespected" (ala Aretha Franklin) the Actives in some drummed up way and we had to wear the scarves everywhere for a week.

The protesters sat in a circle in the growing darkness, about fifty of them, silent, holding candles. I expected to be heckled as I walked by, but no one paid any attention. The candles flickered and danced in the late fall evening. I was acutely aware of a creeping shame, not only because of the ridiculous scarf, but also in the public discrepancy between my outlandish advertisement of my membership in an obviously privileged – and appropriately judged "superficial" – campus club, my sorority, while other students were publicly protesting the rapidly growing number of deaths of young American men in Vietnam and a ghastly war. My heart was torn and uneasy wanting to express support for the soldiers who were getting killed. *They* were not the enemy, but in those days there seemed to be little distinction. As the protests and vigils grew across campus over the following months, Totally Inappropriate Bad Boy Boyfriend became more vocal in his personal protests.

We were a perfect mismatch and he was exactly what I needed at the same time. When I met him that summer he seemed shy and a little sly, someone I knew intuitively was sexually dangerous. He was also obviously poor. Not the right clothes. Scuffed brown shoes. But his eyes looked directly into mine, straight into places I was uncomfortable being seen. I was still officially and technically High School Boyfriend Bob's girlfriend so I did not want to "encourage" this guy, at the same time I was uncomfortably intrigued and definitely attracted.

We met again a few weeks later at the beginning of term when I was going through my breakup crisis with High School Boyfriend Bob and trying to reach my parents in Panama to transfer to University of Texas. Totally Inappropriate Bad Boy Boyfriend was part of the BSU (Baptist Student Union) crowd, and I realized he was quite popular – older than other students (after switching majors several times – another red flag) and we started dating soon after the term started. And yes, he did turn out to be dangerous, and quite inexperienced in other ways. We were sexual magnets. I don't believe we ever had a string of more than a few weeks together before we'd break up and then be back together in another few weeks. It was crazy making, and he was addictive. He was also changing right before my eyes.

He became outspoken as an anti-war protester and began going to meetings and events on campus, protests, vigils, sit-ins, that made me extremely uncomfortable. He dropped out of school to figure out what to do about it all. An older, college drop-out, Vietnam War protester, Conscientious Objector. That's a perfect fit for The Colonel's Daughter, right? He'd officially dropped out. Was there any more damning label in those days than College Drop Out? How had I learned to be so arrogant? He still hung around the BSU and the campus and we still dated and broke up and got back together and broke up and got back together and broke up and got back together. He had no prospects in my eyes. It was a dead-end relationship.

I've never been any good at ending relationships. I see that now. I don't want people to think badly of me for whatever reason, so it dragged on. Looking back at all those should-have-been endings that eased into messy rides into the sunset, I think I am so conflict avoidant that I can't bear the idea of telling someone I'm through. Most of them should have been three dates and a handshake goodbye.

The pursuit of the Conscientious Objector status quest was in full swing with Totally Inappropriate Bad Boy Boyfriend when I was introduced to a young man from Lubbock who was a West Pointer, the Company Commander of a cadet I'd met in Panama the summer before. You remember my telling you about the Panama Summers and the steady stream of cadets, right? You've already heard about the Lubbock boy I was introduced to: tall with the build of the athlete he was and considered good looking in some circles in that rough West Texas way; disciplined enough to get into West Point and play college football at the top level; always presentable and neatly dressed; yes sir/yes ma'am; goal oriented; upstanding/Christian, from a "good family." The timing was good. I felt increasingly anxious about my life in general, conflicted over both the world situation, the draft, the war, and Totally Inappropriate Bad Boy Boyfriend. During long-distance phone calls between Lubbock and West Point I asked him a few years after we met why he was attracted to me. "You've got good bullshit. You know how to carry on a conversation and keep it interesting." That critique left me disappointed, but in those days that was considered intimate conversation. For him, I was a perfect profile fit for a young West Point lieutenant's potential wife. Somewhere in the back of my mind an unspoken private mantra began to form that silently predicted the many years of relationships ahead: Always too much, but never enough. It never occurred to either of us we had nothing in common other than the fact I was raised in a Baptist and military family and he was a Baptist and West Pointer. It never came up.

If only it had.

He came to Panama that next summer. What if he hadn't? We met. We danced. We dined at my house hosted by my parents. It was the beginning of the story of how I would end up an Ex-Texan, divorced three times, ultimately living in Wimberley forty-three years later, and figuring out how I got here. Everything was going to plan. But whose?

What if it hadn't?

Trains I've Missed

Music and Lyrics by Walt Wilkins

Here's to the trains I missed, the loves I lost
The bridges I burned, the rivers I never crossed
Here's to the call I didn't hear, the signs I didn't heed
The roads I didn't take, the maps that I just wouldn't read

It's a big old world but I've found my way
And the hell and the hurt lead me straight to you
Here's to the trains I missed

I've been a clown, I've been a fool,
and I pushed on every chance
I crossed too many lines trying to crawl out of God's hands
There were stones I didn't throw, and hearts I didn't break
And a little hope that I held onto
with each silver shining thread of faith

It's a big old world but I've found my way
And the hell and the hurt lead me straight to this
Here's to the trains I missed

Here's to this place I've found, the love I've known
The earth and the sky here that I call home
Here's to the things that I believe are bigger than me
And the moments I find myself right where I want to be

It's a big old world but I've found my way
And the hell and the hurt lead me straight to it
Here's to the trains I missed

9 – TWO BY TWO AND DO SI DO

Dancing's just a conversation between two people. Talk to me.

~ Justin Matisse (Harry Connick, Jr.) to Birdee Pruitt
(Sandra Bullock) in the movie "Hope Floats"

I fell in love with square dancing in Miss Gibney's sixth grade class. It started out as one of our activities on winter or rainy days when we couldn't go out to the playground and play kickball, or tetherball, or dodge ball. This was a relief from the brutality of the stronger boys displaying their affections for a girl by slamming the ball as hard as they could into her back or legs. A sign of young love for sure.

During these rainy indoor recess days every class in the sixth grade was introduced to the same portfolio of classic folk or square dances: The Oyster and the Pearl, The Virginia Reel, Turkey in the Straw. I loved the orderliness and predictability of the steps, the assignment of various partners by virtue of the dance protocol. The luck of the draw would sometimes give me Bobby Hughes, who I had a big crush on and was my first kiss a year later in a laundry room off another 7th grader's rec room. Or Eric Brently who was all arms and legs and shy and wore glasses that could never quite stay on his nose, whose hands were always a little sweaty, but kind. I knew the orderliness of the square dance would guarantee I'd only be with my "assigned" partner for a short portion of the dance. Off we'd go. Sometimes we crossed hands at our hips and skipped around the circle or across the square two by two. Sometimes we'd all move into the center and then back out again. Each dance had a pattern.

The best move was the Do Si Do. With arms crossed at shoulder height I'd face my partner passing right shoulders and without turning around step back to back then back up passing left shoulders until I was in front of my partner again. It required focus because for at least part of the move I couldn't actually *see* my partner. I had to believe if I followed the steps I wouldn't crash back to back with my partner. And, for the most part, we didn't. It was my adult life in microcosm: if I follow the steps I'll end up in the right place with the right partner.

A strange thing happened in that sixth grade class while we fidgeted through the moves and made fun of each other, and particularly Miss Gibney. We got good. I mean, really good, at the whole thing. Somewhere along the line we learned the steps and began to find pleasure in our various squares and circles, relying on each other to know our steps and be ready for the next move individually, with our partner, with our group.

Getting good became fun and suddenly a source of power. Our class was paraded around, by the request of other teachers and even other students, to display our prowess. We took it seriously and showed it, which only added to our legend. On days we knew we'd be "touring" to another class, I wore my favorite white blouse and dirndl skirt made by my mother and made sure Daddy polished my red Mary Janes. The boys would look presentable, even if that only meant a tucked-in shirt. The day we performed our signature dance, The Irish Washerwoman, at the seventh grade assembly in front of all four of the classes at one time, in our creaky auditorium always smelling of sweat and old sneakers, we later had the nerve to cut in the lunch line knowing we were kings and queens of the school on that day — untouchable.

My introduction to square dancing and the excitement it brought and the chance to hold hands with the Bobby Hughses and Eric Brentleys of the world, even fleetingly, in a grand, or more probably not so grand, right and left, was also my introduction to boys and the potential for the two-by-two couple thing in life. With square dancing though, the actual two-by-two thing never lasted too long. Just like the Irish Washerwoman reel, I was always on the cusp of changing partners and dancing off down the line. Square dancing made sense to me because it was all about patterns, about relationships, about moving forward, back, sideways, apart, touching hands and not. I don't recall much of a role for the single person in square dancing. That would come twenty-five years later watching a line of women dance in the movie *Urban Cowboy*. Forty years since that began, single lines of women are still forming at weddings, and often in the dance halls here in Texas. For some reason, watching those lines makes me sad in some deep place. I'm not ready to go there yet.

I am a helpless meaning maker, inveterate relationship organizer of any category of components. It's what made me a good consultant: coming into a complex situation or organization cold and able to quickly discern patterns and categories. But then, I've had over forty years to look for them.

I never had much cause to look at the state of Being Single and now I wonder about that. Like most things in life that seem obvious, this thing's not as simple as it appears and looks different depending on my point of view age-wise, marriage-wise, culture-wise, and even geography-wise. It is not all the same. Single at twenty-six was not the same thing as single at forty was definitely not the same thing as single at sixty-four. Single at twenty-six and forty felt natural, transitional. Single at sixty-four has a telescoping effect where there are fewer years looking ahead than behind. Single in New York City just isn't the same as being single in a small town. In New York it's easier to blend in because there are a lot of us, and no one really gives a damn if you're single outside of Jewish mothers of both daughters and sons.

I have been working on a taxonomy of sorts, an intellectual plaything, a matrix, something I love to do to sort connections among my own relationships, experiences, questions, and confusions. I did this all the time in my professional life, either using my tried and true and useful friends, like the Johari Window, which provides a framework of Things that Are Known or Unknown to Me or Others, Conscious or Unconscious, or making up new ones. During my years working with General Electric, we often used a matrix the celebrated CEO Jack Welch created for evaluating leadership talent: Makes the Numbers/Lives the Values/Yes/No. Or the well-known and very useful prioritizing tool: The Payoff Matrix: Easy to Do/Hard to Do/High Impact/Low Impact. And dozens of others. They are fun to make up and emerge everywhere when I begin to think that way.

A good friend, an elegant woman and friend of over twenty years, told me about an eHarmony first date she'd been on years back. Nice enough man, age appropriate, but when the topic came around to being single, he said, "I've been single for four years. How about you." After a longish pause she replied, "Twenty-nine years." Longer pause. Longer awkward silence.

"Single" is not the same for everyone and in many ways, a useless term. Clearly anyone can feel single whether legally bound by a piece of paper, or deeply partnered or coupled without one. There are different levels and sources of

Singleness, which generate varying reactions from others and implications for anyone, including me.

The Widowed

Being widowed generates the highest level of respect and sympathy. Assumptions are that it must have been a good relationship since it lasted, no matter how long. When on a date, the conversation about the marriage is spoken in soft, sympathetic tones. Very few people, although I have known a couple, always women, say something to the effect of, "I'm glad that son-of-a-bitch is gone. He made my life a living hell." Once while I was working in a New York City downtown branch in the Consumer Sector of the bank, I saw a woman, still dressed in black, suddenly rage at the top of her lungs at the poor fellow at the banker's desk in the lobby, sweeping everything off the banker's desk onto the floor, screaming for all of Wall Street to hear, "That son of a bitch told me we were one step away from being broke. He NEVER let me spend a cent!!" She had just learned he was, in fact, quite wealthy but kept her nearly penniless for reasons of his own. But that's an exception, of course. At least I hope so.

The Divorced

In talking with a divorced person, at least at first, there is usually some sympathy, probably not too much respect depending on the circumstances and the divorced person's anger-victim reading on the emotional thermometer. Divorced, who knows? It can happen to any of us and probably has. Twice, well, okay, in today's world not that unusual. Three times or more? Dicey, considering 3% of the population has been married three times or more, and 74% of third marriages end in divorce. I was taken aback when I read that statistic. While being divorced three times is not something I'm proud of or talk about, I really thought there were more of us out there. Clunk, clunk. The sound of rubies dropping.

Then there is the subset of **Divorced: The Dumped**

Now this one's complicated, for sure. "I was blindsided." "I didn't see it coming." "Just like that, it was over." "He had a mid-life crisis." "He met someone younger." I have been a Dumpee, but now with hindsight, not so blindsided and not so unexpected. First reaction to Dumpees is sympathy tinged with prurient curiosity. Was it for a secretary? A pool guy? Someone with more money? And the perennial "Was she younger?" Interest dwindles as time goes on. Sympathy dwindles from friends, new acquaintances, colleagues, or oneself. It can buckle under the heavy lifting of torquing among "What's wrong with her?" "What did she do to make him/her dump him/her?" "There must be another part of her personality we don't see," most often never spoken but probably thought. It can morph quickly and damagingly to "What's wrong with *me*?" Compounding this mess is where the dumping occurs in the divorce continuum. Having been a two-time dumper as well as a Dumpee, I can tell you, it's a mess.

When I became newly and truly single for the first time in my life, one of the things that surprised me was how many of my very happily long-term married women friends said, some ruefully, most with tongue firmly in cheek, something to the effect of:

"I love (fill in the blank), but if something ever happened to him, I'd never get married again."

"I love (fill in the blank), but if he could just magically disappear, I'd be okay with that."

"Sometimes I envy you and your freedom – not how you got it – but just your freedom."

As I write this I have been officially, legally divorced, and single – this time – for a decade. Writing these words feels like I'm writing about someone else. It's an otherworldly, out-of-body experience. Everyone assumed I would mark time for a little while until I found another relationship and ultimately remarry. It's what I do. Granted, I have been in a couple of longer-term relationships – one with Totally Inappropriate Bad Boy Boyfriend forty-two years after our college romp. It lasted a couple of years and almost every moment I felt the same ambivalence I did during out college years and ultimately broke it off, (which has never been my MO except with him – okay, one other) for many of the same reasons I did the first time. He was married and divorced three times as well. We often mused out loud together if we weren't suited to marriage, or if marriage wasn't suited to us, or if we just didn't find the right "fit." We were driven to come up with an explanation to justify why it had not "taken." I still wonder about all that, but I no longer start from the baseline of marriage as the default. "Swing your partner round and round. Bow to your left. Bow to your right. Allemande left and grand right and left!" "Move On," as the Stephen Sondheim song goes in his musical *Sunday in the Park with George.*

Then there is Philosophical Divorce: "It was for the best. We'll always be friends;" Ambivalent Divorce: "I'll always love him/her, we just couldn't live together but it's best for the kids…I think"); and Bitter Divorce: "I put him/her through school and he does *this*?" "He left me for a younger woman/my best friend/his secretary/man!" Yes, that still happens. I'll admit, I (thankfully) never gave into that – bitterness.

Perhaps the hardest to understand is just plain old Heartbroken Divorce. ("He/She just left."). At least that's how I see it. I will admit to Heartbroken Divorce. I wonder what His Nib's one-liner was about me. I have my suspicions. It would have been easier to accept with a younger woman, best friend's wife, secretary scenario. Having someone do whatever they needed to do to get away from me as fast as possible at whatever cost was a psychological wrecking ball, leaving me desperately craving that one-liner regardless of how true or false it felt to me. Something. Anything. My mind kept spiraling downward until I had to stop.

I am reminded of West Point Starter Husband's explanation when asked, "What happened?" when we split up after a few years. His answer was simple. Succinct. "She freaked out over women's lib." As jejune and dismissive as his one liner was, in some respects it was true if not well expressed. We were married in June (of course). By February of the following year we were living in the New York Hudson Valley at West Point. Like so many places at that time, especially academia of just about any type, it was a period of social and political upheaval. West Point was a cauldron of intellectual fever on the social sciences side where, unbeknownst to me, the feminist move-ment was in full swing. Out of boredom from attending the requisite Commanding Officer's wife's teas, complete with wrist-length white gloves, and my secretarial job at Marine Midland Bank outside the West Point gates in the small town of Highland Falls, I sought a glimmer of hope of something else in the bright light of completely new thinking of the women's movement.

I enrolled in classes for a Counselor Education program offered on post at West Point. Most of the men on post opted for the MBA program so most of my classmates were women. Army Wives. Smart. Ambitious. The women in my classes came from the larger West Point community. One was the wife of a Belgian military attaché posted there. Gwen already had a full-time position as an Intake Coordinator at the large local county mental health complex close to West Point. I was intimidated by her and how we ended up being friends is still a mystery. Gwen took herself, her work, and her education, all independent of her status as an Army wife, seriously. Starter Husband and I got to know them as a couple as a result of the two of us being classmates.

We arrived at their home for dinner one Christmas, their Christmas tree blazing with real burning candles as was the custom in Wilhelm's hometown in Belgium. Starter Husband nervously watched, making slow covert sweeps with his eyes around the room for a fire extinguisher or at least the nearest exit. It was beautiful – and terrifying.

While sitting around their formal white table-clothed dinner table one night sipping the remainder of a remarkable red wine, Gwen asked me, "Have we ever savored champagne together?"

Startled, and putting aside my starched and pressed white napkin with the European lace trim, placing it next to the sterling silver fork, I responded, "Oh, yes, Gwen. We've savored champagne together many times!"

"No," she insisted, "*sabered* champagne."

"I guess not," I confessed, not having any idea what she meant.

"Let's do it! Wilhelm! Get your sword! I'll get the goblets!"

The four of us moved to their front yard where Wilhelm hand-ed Gwen a bottle of (quite good) champagne. She settled it in the frozen ground then picked up the two sterling silver West Point goblets she'd brought outside. "Stand back," Wilhelm admonished in his heavy Dutch accent. Shivering, we stood back, except for Gwen who knelt unnervingly close to the bottle on the ground. Using his West Point saber, Wilhelm took a long, slicing upward sweep just below the neck of the bottle, ending with a practiced twist of the wrist at the right moment, sending the neck of the bottle, complete with the intact cork, flying across the yard. Gwen was poised at the freshly decap-itated bottle, scooping up the bubbly streaming into the sterling silver West Point goblets. Stunning. Breathtaking. Unnerving.[11]

At other times Gwen would talk about her real work in a real office, with real clients, and a real paycheck. I intuited that spending my days in the backroom of the small Marine Midland Bank outside the West Point gates with a pencil and a big fat oversized blue cap of an eraser flipping through the backside of checks looking for signatures didn't really count as work – at least for me. Then one miraculous day, after taking the Civil Service Exam, my number came up and I was assigned to the West Point Engineering Division. At last. A civil service secret-arial job at West Point! The brass ring.

Each civil service division at West Point had a senior GS (Government Service) level Director and a military officer partner to run point on specific military related issues of the business. My civilian boss, Mr. Blair, was one of the gentlest and kindest men I've ever known. He saw in me something I couldn't see in myself – a bright, sociable, efficient, hard-working twenty-four year-old. He also appreciated my

Olivetti-Underwood Typist Award of Merit from my high school days, along with my Texas UIL (University Inter-scholastic League – kind of like academic intramurals across the whole state) Region 4 typing finalist designation. Mr. Blair was respectful and pleasant and enjoyed the fact that my husband was a football coach. All the men in the division, and they were all men, liked that. Seems it gave them bragging rights of some kind to someone. I never knew what kind or to whom. I confess I did enjoy feeding them occasional insider information about the team and coaches, such as tidbits from some scouting trips my husband routinely filled me in on.

Mr. Blair trusted me and gave me larger responsibilities than my GS-3 classification (about the lowest there is) warranted. He never once asked me the question that the other engineers and others asked me over the years, other than the usual, "What does your husband think about you working?" The other question they wanted answered was "Do you read what you're typing or just type it?" I don't understand that question no matter what angle or positive spin I put on it. Maybe it's my naturally curious Gemini mind always absorbing everything, from the specs I'm typing for the repair of ship locks in the Panama Canal, to the width of the PVC required to replace the plumbing in the post houses. Nota bene: Yes, world. I always know what I'm typing.

That "'fraid to miss something" or FMS Lobe as it was ascribed to me one time, had real repercussions on the day I was typing some new specs for the cadet barracks. At home that evening over boxed tuna noodle casserole and sweet tea I happened to mention the interesting work I'd done that day.

"Guess what I was working on today?" I ventured. "I've been typing the specs to add additional electrical outlets in the barracks for the new women cadets." Cadets are not allowed to bring private property when they arrive for their Plebe, or freshman year, so the government would have to issue Clairol Hot Rollers, new on the market, to all women cadets when they arrived. The engineering specs called for installing additional electrical outlets in every dorm room to accommodate the new appliance. In addition, the specs called for reconfiguring the barracks closet to allow for hanging full length "dress blues" evening gowns. From the days of the first cadet in 1802, these same closets were configured for men's shirts, dress blues "blouses" (as the jackets are officially known), and trousers. As I shared all this fascinating information to great dramatic effect, West Point Starter Husband stood up and looked at me for a few long seconds, turned and walked out of the room. He did not speak to me before going to bed, as if somehow I was personally responsible for this unholy, egregious, cataclysmic, tectonic shift of events in moral and military history. All this time I was under the misconception I didn't have any personal power, in our relationship or the world. I guess I was wrong since the clackity clack of my typewriter keys could apparently, double-handedly, change the course of military and American history.

Attending classes in the master's program week after week for over a year and a half produced seismic personal shifts. I studied psychology, human development, and educational theories and statistics, all of which fascinated me. I also learned about the current social tides of the day trending towards the encounter group movement and the famous Esalen Institute Program on the west coast. I devoured information about The National Training Laboratory (NTL) in Bethel, Maine, born out of post-World War II research into group dynamics, racism, and social justice. A few years later I would meet the brilliant, compassionate, and very handsome Elliot Aronson, one of the founders of Social Psychology and a hero of mine at NTL. His groundbreaking text, *The Social Animal,* became a second Bible to me. NTL, its programs, research, and workshops were a passion of the Chief of Psychology at the West Point Hospital who taught the Theories of Psychology course in my program. Later, I would learn he was passionate about me as well.

I knew one day I would attend the NTL Basic Human Interaction Program, which was an initial two-week intensive encounter group. I couldn't wait. In the meantime, I soaked up Gestalt, Rogerian, Eriksonian, Jungian, Freudian, and Tavistock psychology theories of development and treatment modalities faster than I could read the texts. I participated in T-Groups (sensitivity training groups) run by the West Point psychologist faculty member. I couldn't get enough of it. Or him, apparently. A year later West Point Starter Husband and I decided to split. He'd had enough of my rebellion, once being admonished by the head football coach to "keep your woman in line," and returned to West Texas and Texas Tech, ultimately becoming a Western History Museum Director of several iconic museums and a renowned western museum, art expert, and author.

When he berated me that evening for causing difficulties for his West Point career, I knew I was never going back to Texas because by then I couldn't imagine a life there anymore. Just a few months before, his parents had offered us a run-down adobe house forty miles from Lubbock, which is hardly anywhere to begin with, which they owned. We were "invited" to fix up the 'ol homestead while my husband left the military and got his graduate degree in Western Museum Science at Texas Tech. I would no longer be a West Point Wife, my only thread of positive connection in the marriage at that point. My appetite for a larger, deeper, more exciting world without dust devils and sandstorms had been triggered. To be fair, we had gone into the marriage with a clear contract and path. He would be the one with the exciting career and I would be the one to support him and the career, be that "asset." The two of us had indeed become one and it was him. I was the one who changed the terms. I stayed in New York in a new job at the Orange County Mental Health Clinic, thanks to Gwen. It was a turbulent and thrilling time.

After the breakup with West Point Starter Husband, I was visiting my parents in San Antonio, sitting with my father on the bed in my old bedroom, weeping. The familiar colors of the Lincoln log pattern quilt I was sitting on was made by my mother and grandmother, an activity they shared together for many years. It offered familiarity but no comfort.

"I'm twenty-six and don't have a home," I hiccupped through tears.

"Honey, you always have a home here for however long you want or need it," my dad said.

What I wanted to say was, "That doesn't really count. I am an adult and I'm supposed to be on my own, in my own home, with my own husband." Not a single alternative scenario ever occurred to me, like go get a job I loved, live somewhere I wanted to live. Instead, I said, "What am I going to say when people ask me what happened?"

"You will tell them," my dad said, "what I told your mother to say when she asked me that same question: Tell them you left the son-of-a-bitch." That seemed rather harsh to me. I didn't think badly of my husband. I was no longer able to live in the world we'd created together.

The West Point psychologist who taught my Theories of Psychology graduate course eventually became Hyphen-Husband, as he would become labeled in my ex-husband canon. He was not only a clinical psychologist-academic-professor-therapist, but he was also a musician-singer-songwriter, manic-depressive, the latter going undiagnosed for decades. We lasted twenty years, though. He was manic and high strung when he wasn't depressed. Prolific with words, he taught me everything I ever learned about contemporary popular music. He took me to dozens of Broadway musicals and theater plays during those twenty years where I learned the Broadway canon of Stephen Sondheim, Andrew Lloyd Webber, and Stephen Schwartz. We went to concerts held in small dusty primitive venues like hay lofts or local high school gyms to hear Jackson Brown, Emmy Lou Harris, Don McLean, Paul Winter, and dozens of artists just beginning their careers. I learned the first Tuesday in October was the High Holy Day of album releases and accompanied him to Tower Records in Manhattan or the Nanuet, New Jersey Mall, to be among the first to buy an album from some highly touted badass like Springsteen, or Simon and Garfunkel's newest, as well as obscure, to me anyway, groups like Toad The Wet Sprocket, Fairport Convention, and hundreds of others. Together we sang his original compositions and an excellent musical he wrote, none of which ever saw a professional recording. He took me to Ireland, the first of my subsequent dozens of trips over many years. We rode the Ferris wheel in Paris in the Tuileries one New Year's Eve and ate Croque Monsiuers. We were determined to catch the first showing on the first day of blockbuster movie releases like *Jaws*, *Star Wars*, *Indiana Jones*, and *E. T.* He was fun. He took me and my growing ambition to create a professional career as seriously as he took his.

And he was, I learned very late in our relationship, completely unfaithful from the beginning. Honor your partner and do-si-do? Not quite. He was, by his own wry admission and in the theories of Carl Jung, a classic Puer Aeternus, the ultimate Peter Pan, the boy who wouldn't grow up. As Maya Angelou famously said, "When people show you who they are, believe them the first time." The first time I met him he had wine stains on the front of his white medical coat at the hospital. Twenty years later I left him. It was only the second time in my life I'd made a clean break. Maybe I was learning.

When you've been married and divorced three times, the sheer management of exes takes some strategizing. It becomes an inconvenient necessity and can be accomplished through intention or default or a little of both. Years of hindsight have given me one additional lens for categorization:

Starter-Husband: *Pretend it never happened.* Do nothing ever again, have no contact whatsoever, with or without malice. It's like an annulment without the interference of the church

Hyphen-Husband - *Least Favorite Husband/Most Favorite Ex*: Recognize the marriage ended poorly but was not a total loss, like the way a car is totaled after an accident. Over time acknowledge to yourself and each other that you are much better exes than spouses. The one thing that's made all the difference in the almost three decades of divorce from Hyphen-Husband is that, after telling me he finally got medications for his various conditions, late, but not too late, he apologized for his part in the destruction of the relationship, for not being a better husband, and for the hurt he caused. He's still a little nuts, now known as the eccentric old man in the town where he lives who writes thrice-weekly letters to the editor of the local paper on every conceivable global or local issue, but I admire his activism. His eccentricities don't affect me anymore, and at least he wants to share them with me. He's always been interesting, a quality that is a fatal attraction for me. I still care about him.

His-Nibs: *Most Favorite Husband/Least Favorite Ex:* The years we had together were composed of day-to-day deep satisfactions. I used to tell friends the quality of my life increased fifty percent when he walked through the door. And I meant it. When he left me, he also became a terrible ex. All I ever wanted was a simple "I'm sorry." Not an "I'm sorry" about anything I may have perceived as injury he inflicted, or that the marriage didn't last, but a "sorry" for acknowledging how much pain I was in. That was all, really. I'm still waiting.

As I sit in the dugout of life after my third strike out at bat, I cast about for other possible explanations for how I ended up off the marriage team after being prepared for it my whole life. At this point I had no definitive answers, but some plotlines were emerging.

Now I sit in Wimberley, Texas, in the gentle, rolling, sweet, lush hills of The Hill Country, far from New York, Santa Barbara, Connecticut, or Paris, looking back on the dance of life and, certainly, the dance of love. My life so far really has been a dance. From a distance, the changing of partners looks like the Grand Allemande of a square dance. Right over left over right. Inside. Outside. Insider. Outsider. Changing, not really going anywhere but changing for the novelty of the next hand in the grand circle and square, the line of dance, round and round. Just keep moving, but not really, always coming around to where I began.

The playwright Miranda July put it this way:

*Sometimes I would make left turns all the way around a block,
and when I returned to the original intersection, I would feel
disappointed to find all the drivers were new. It wasn't like a
square dance where you miraculously ended up with your
original partner, laughing and feeling giddily relieved to find
him after dancing with everyone else in the world. Instead, they
swung around and kept going, some people were at work by
now, or halfway to the airport.*

Miraculously ending up with your original partner. Imagine that.
But give me credit. Those partners have all been creative, interesting men, some of them even coming teeteringly close to the
many truly brilliant women I've been fortunate to know. Maybe
next go 'round. Do si do, allemande left, and onward. Always
Two by Two. Maybe not, and that's okay, too.

I've always had the boots, but I can't seem to hold on to the
partner no matter how fast or slow they spin me.

Single Supplement – Random Thoughts

By Chick Morgan ©2023

Single surcharge
Singles bar – more dangerous by far
Kraft singles – individually wrapped and always more expensive
Single women always suspect
Single men always welcome
With couple friends a 3rd or 5th wheel. How fun.
Like Noah – 2 x 2's the way towards existence
1 x 1 the way to extinction
Single malt good. Double malt (not my fault) better
Single shot
Single file
Hit single
The cheese stands alone.

Comings and Goings

10 – ALL BETS ARE OFF

Everything's backwards in Texas
That's why I'm looking younger every day

~ Chick Morgan, unpublished lyric ©2023

Sometime during the Great Shitstorm I must have made the leap from "I have to live somewhere" to deciding it would be Texas, at least for a while. Looking back on that time I try hard to remember how that came about. The path to that decision was as crooked as the streets in downtown San Antonio formed by cows on the legendary cattle drives more than a century ago.

The truthful answer to the question "How did you get here to Wimberley?" seemed pretty simple: 1) My mother died, my daddy had increasing dementia, and I wanted to spend more time with him as long as he knew me. 2) My brother and sister-in-law lived about fifty minutes away from San Antonio where Daddy lived in a health facility. I could have a landing pad nearby without having to live in San Antonio. San Antonio is a fascinating, diverse, and culturally rich city but weighted down with the baggage of too much of my past, a lot of it pleasant, but my past, nonetheless. Some of those bags are my happy childhood and teenage years which I'd manage to shake off and retool into a different me over the last forty plus years. It felt like going backwards. All of it: geography, family, friends, history, relationships. Nobody in Texas knew – really knew – who I was today. How could they? I'd left them all behind. Deliberately.

There is another part to my story that I didn't bother to share with anyone. My story of good daughterly self-sacrifice was self-serving and not completely true. During what would turn out to be the last month or so of my travels before reluctantly settling into Wimberley, not knowing that was where I would end up, I was in the final stages of signing a consulting contract for high six figures a year for several years, or as long as I wanted. Because of multiple and various laws, mostly international, fulfilling the contract would mean I'd be living in Saudi Arabia for two months at a time and then back to the states for two months before going back to Saudi Arabia. I could return to the same location or continue my travels with various landing pads around the country or, possibly, the world. I could get that cottage in Ireland or a beachfront house in Thailand, or a small stone house in the Italian countryside. It was going to be the perfect rhythm of timing so that I could attend to some so-called "medical tourism" for that face lift or liposuction if I chose and recover before returning to Saudi Arabia again. It didn't have to be somewhere in the US. It just needed to not be in Saudi Arabia. I could make Texas one of those come-and-go places, see my dad occasionally, but stay on the move, which frankly, I'd grown fond of and was energized by. This set up with Saudi Arabia would be the perfect structure to live any-where and everywhere I had the inkling. I wouldn't have time to get involved with anything in any community other than on a superficial basis as I'd have no time to meet people, do things socially, let alone make friends. That was just fine. What I wanted and needed, or so I thought, was a completely different kind of life, involved with what little family I do have, and still with some pattern of care for my dad, relieving my brother and sister-in-law.

It was a great project in Saudi, a career capstone. It meant organizationally restructuring the largest university for women in Saudi Arabia to accommodate a new age. Crown Prince Mohammed bin Salman, or MBS for short, had become the darling of the media with stories of how he was modernizing the Kingdom, especially for women. The magnitude and grandiosity of the university and the project to reinvent its organizational and academic structures and programs was one of the highlights. Huge in scale, limitless in funding, wide open to put into practice everything my team and I had been creating and teaching with our corporate clients for twenty years, it was breathtaking in scope. If I had still been in my marriage, participating at the required level and scope would not have been remotely possible, the upside of being dumped. I was free in every sense of the word, and, miracle of miracles, like the proverbial Biblical manna from heaven, it arrived out of thin air at a time I was feeling acutely vulnerable financially. The project would provide financial freedom and independence for the rest of my life, something that has a more specific end game at sixty-four than I'd imagined at thirty. As an extra bonus, this project would go a long way in wiping the dirt off my boots of a heartbreaking experience and help me start my new life in a big way. And since we're being truthful here, it would also be a big in-your-face response to my "inability to generate income," a refrain I dearly wanted him to regret making, kitchen to die for or not.

I was reflecting on the fortuitous timing of this project one evening at the home of my friend Sharon and her husband, Mike. For several months I'd been living in a space in their home providing me a base of operations and mailing address. Sharon and Mike, like everyone I knew who knew about the upcoming Saudi project, were trying to talk me out of going as a very, very bad idea. In hindsight it probably was. Dangerous they said! A single woman in her sixties jetting back and forth and flitting around the world alone! You could be kidnapped or thrown into prison or even killed, they said! Probably true.

At the time I thought they were exhibiting very small-minded thinking as I had been in potentially dangerous work and travel positions most of my adult life, such as flying to Russia alone at a time it was still the Soviet Union two days after Yeltsin stood on the tanks in Red Square; or sitting at a public park in then Czechoslovakia acting as if my colleague and I were on a picnic, waiting for a contact to arrive to do some business, all the while watching the police with their German Shepherds repeatedly stroll by; sitting in my first class seat in a plane taking off from Bangkok airport, watching the tanks roll onto the runway at the start of a coup. My modus operandi seemed to be to miss the actual danger by a day or two but experience the frisson of potential danger in its wake. I yearned to be in real action. It drove my parents, and various husbands, nuts.

I was sitting at Sharon and Mike's kitchen table with their friend, Other Mike, who I'd met over the years. I knew Other Mike and his wife as friends with whom I'd traveled on an island jaunt with Sharon and Mike. Over the years His Nibs and I had been together with them in gatherings in Connecticut, including several days of evacuation during Hurricane Sandy, along with our ancient, infirmed, three-legged cat. Other Mike is a financial guy, planner and consultant. I was going on enthu-siastically about the Saudi project and the financial structure for it when he burst my bubble.

"You know, you can't live in Connecticut when this contract comes through," he said, swirling his very good cabernet from our host's wine cellar around and around in the very good crystal stemless wine glass. "In addition to the federal taxes, the state taxes are going to eat you alive." Having filed taxes jointly in Connecticut with His Nibs for years, I knew what he was talking about. "And," he continued, moving the chips and hot crab dip around on the elegant handmade lace tablecloth as he looked straight at me reading my mind, "you can't live in California, either. Santa Barbara is out, too for the same reason." I admit, I had been quietly fantasizing off and on about a tri-coastal arrangement among Connecticut, Santa Barbara, and Texas (where we do actually have a coast, the Gulf Coast.) But I concluded I had no desire to be anywhere near my soon- to-be ex. "No matter where in the world you end up spending your alternate two months, you'll be paying exorbitant taxes. You need to live somewhere that doesn't have a state income tax. That will help some."

"Okay," I replied, "So where, then?"

Florida!

No way.

Nevada doesn't have a state income tax.

You must be kidding.

How about Sitka?

I knew Sitka was in Alaska. I also knew it was Other Mike's way of messing with me. I didn't know much about Alaska but I did know that a single woman friend of mine who's lived there many years declared it a place, when we were talking about men, "where the odds are good but the goods are odd." No thank you.

He tried one more time. "Arizona?" expertly swishing the wine in the crystal wine glass, counterclockwise. "Dream on," I thought to myself. I sighed and poured myself another glass of cabernet.

I looked up at Sharon, catching her eye as she sipped on her own wine. "You know," I mused. "I seem to recall from somewhere that Texas doesn't have a state income tax." It may be the only redeeming social value for living there, I thought at the time, if you don't hunt or live on a steady diet of high school and college football, or you're not in the military, high tech, or cattle ranching. Even though I'd been head cheerleader in high school and attended all the football games all four years at Texas Tech (home *and* away), I had not watched a game in forty-three years as an absentee Texan and hadn't missed a minute of it.

Sharon and I looked at each other. The penny dropped. This could be the short-term answer I needed. Texas ticked the boxes. No state income tax. It was familiar. I had family and friends in Texas and quite a bit of history, maybe too much. I could use it as a base to be with Daddy on a regular basis between stints in Saudi Arabia. The answer had been staring at me all along, but I had not wanted to see it. So there it was. I might just have easily used the Biblical reference, "It is finished," but won't, even though that's how it felt. My life, as I knew it in every aspect, would be finished, or at least on hold for a while.

I had been traveling for the better part of five months with intermittent trips to San Antonio and Wimberley before moving on to my next road trip destination. The day before I'd been on the phone with a grad school alum and consulting colleague from Switzerland. Both she and her husband were closely related to Swiss banking families and my friend lived in a beautiful mansion in Geneva, also spending time at their chateau in the Alps. Karolina is stunningly beautiful, blindingly smart, and had been inviting His Nibs and me to come for a visit ever since we'd met in graduate school. Of course, he never wanted to go and always had legitimate work reasons to put her off. During our catch up call the day before, Karolina invited me once again, encouraging me strongly and emphasizing how great it would be to spend time together that wasn't structured around academic sessions. She wanted to show me Geneva and the Alps. She also had a work meeting in Zurich. We could take the train and meet up with a good friend of hers there for dinner who she knew I'd love. I agreed, but did not commit, wondering how in the world I'd be able to rustle up the cost of an international airline ticket right then.

A few days later the recorded message broke into my thoughts for the umpteenth time as I held the phone. "Thank you for calling Bank of America. All of our representatives are busy. We will get to your call as soon as possible. We appreciate your patience."

I had decided that morning to take His Nibs off our corporate bank account. The business was mine in every way except his name on the documents. I had built the consulting business over 30 years. They were my clients, and it was my work around the world that constituted the core of the business. He never had any involvement in the business other than to enjoy the side benefits of the travel which were a deductible business expense, of course. It had been a good system. During one of our lame "mediation" sessions, a process which in our case, or at least for me, had been a total waste of time, I offered to buy him out of the business for one dollar and he agreed. I fished through my wallet and found a single wrinkled dollar bill, slapping it down on the table in front of me and the attorneys. In return, he wrote me a receipt on the damp napkin provided for my water glass in the attorney's office, asking the two attorneys to notarize, which they did. This exchange prompted my urgency about removing him from the banking documents.

My reverie on the phone was broken by a sudden click, some
background noise, and a cheery voice exclaiming, "Hello, my
name is Ramona. How can I help you today?"

I launched into my story and what I wanted to accomplish.
Ramona listened carefully and walked me through the corporate
bank account and what needed to happen. I was looking at the
most recent statement on-line with her. I saw a notation in the
upper right hand corner labeled World Points, a low six-figure
number beside it.

"What's that number, Ramona?"

"Oh, those are World Points you've accumulated in your name
on the credit card that's associated with this account." Seriously? I was not even aware I/we were accumulating points. "What
are they good for?" I asked her. "Just about anything," she replied. "Hotels, airline miles, specialty items from our catalog."
My mind immediately leapt to the Cartier watches and custom
perfume I'd seen in the Duty Free magazines in many airplane
pockets over many years, neither of which I needed.

"Will I be able to keep those?" I inquired? Her response was
reassuring, "Of course!" Interesting.

"And what do you want to do with your husband's miles?" she
asked.

"What do you mean?" I asked, perplexed.

"If he opened a new account we could transfer these to his new
account…or…" I heard a *long* series of clickety clickety clicks
on her keyboard and then a satisfied, "There! Or…I can just
put them in your account…like…that! How would that be? I

think it's the least we can do," she said with disdain in her voice, "And on the day your mother died!" A slight pause. The number next to the World Points indicator on my account page had swelled significantly.

"Thanks, Ramona. You've been so helpful!" I was becoming more aware and grateful for the power of intermittent angels in my life, but more convinced of the power of sisterhood, even in the unlikeliest situations. I was also more aware how often they were one and the same.

Over my second glass of wine the next evening, one of the remaining Santa Barbara Qupe Syrahs, I thought about my conversation with Ramona the day before. Hmmmm. I wonder. I logged into my account and clicked on the World Points tab and was greeted with various options. I chose Flights. A familiar screen popped up asking for destination, departure and return dates, the usual requests for info. What if… I plugged in JFK to Geneva thinking that would be my most probable departure airport. I clicked on Economy and blinked. The number of miles required was *almost* what was in my account now. So close! It was a good try, I thought, but not to be. Then I saw a notation on the screen. "Would you like to buy extra miles to make up the difference?" Well, yes. Yes, I would at least like to see. I hit the button and was informed that to make up the difference of several thousand miles would cost me $9.16. Was I interested? Hell, yes! Thank you again, Ramona. What a great gift.

Getting there was a different story. At this point in my Year of The Great Shitstorm, it didn't occur to me to get many specifics, like, Karolina's address in Geneva. Even though we'd been on the phone a few days before talking about different date options and agreeing on an arrival date (or so I thought).

I'd just been showing up places and that had worked. But that was before I was flying across the ocean, landing in an airport I'd never been in before, not fluent in any of the three languages of that country, and scrambling to find her address. I knew I must have it somewhere in my phone since we'd been friends for so long. I came up empty after repeated attempts. Who would fly across the Atlantic with a vague idea this was the date we'd agreed on and forget to get the address? In my defense, I honestly thought I had it somewhere in my contacts, and I had tried to confirm the date with her, or at least I thought, with no response. I was confident I would figure it out.

After my conversation with Sharon and the Mikes and before leaving for Geneva I did have the presence of mind to ask my brother and sister-in-law how they would feel about my moving to Wimberley as my next step, to be with them and have a local base to be with Daddy. I honestly didn't know what their reaction might be. My brother and I had not lived in the same state, or even the same country at times, since high school. How would this work, exactly? Would they feel I was encroaching on their turf? Taking advantage of their hospitality? In their customary fashion I was learning to accept, they were very excited. I told them of my plan to go to Switzerland and my sister-in-law planned her real estate attack on my behalf in my absence.

The idea that I might have a home at all was exciting. I had always taken having a home for granted. I am one of the fortunate ones, the privileged ones in so many ways, this assumption I would always have a home being one of those privileges. In my world as an Army kid that home was different from move to move, but it was always our home, my home. You were given the quarters you were given. We didn't get to choose among a Georgian Colonial, Cape Cod, or Mid-Century Modern.

As an adult my home was the place I could put my own things, like pictures, knick knacks, my grandmother's quilt on my bed, a couple wine glasses in the cabinet or on the shelf, wine in the fridge. But this was different. I had never had a home solely on my own. Like many women my age I had moved seamlessly from my parent's home to college dorm to married home. What *did* I want in my home? How did I want to live this new life? What was important to me in terms of space? Who did I see spending time with me there?

I'd always had a mailing address, so learning I needed one to maneuver my day to day life came as a surprise. The government, my bank, my friends and family required an actual address of me, some plot of land or square footage in a building I could point to and say, yes, that's me. See me there? Unlike Van Morrison, they did not appreciate my "gypsy soul," let alone care to rock it.

I'm resourceful. I'll grant myself that. I figured out a way to find the address of the mansion in Geneva, found a taxi, the usual Mercedes Benz, and wound my way up the hillside just above Lake Geneva to the home of Karolina who looked only slightly surprised when I pulled up in the driveway.

My time with Karolina was everything I'd fantasized. Interesting work conversations, lovely meals in surrounding outdoor country restaurant courtyards, a drive through the Alps where we spent a few days in her lovely chateau, a beautiful train trip to Zurich where I met a woman I'm still in close touch with today, some splendid shopping in Geneva, even an interview on her international podcast. Then came a phone call from my brother and sister-in-law that changed the course of The Great Shitstorm.

Karolina and I were working on our laptops on the marble-topped table in the beautiful dining room. My brother called. "Chick, we're looking at a great house here and want you to see it quickly. I'm sending you some FlipCam videos in a minute." In the few days since I'd left Wimberley and flown to Geneva they'd found a house. The videos gave me an almost in-person tour of a charming house, well located in town, in a patio home setting, so no yard to speak of, a very large, covered porch, a wood burning fireplace, and everything else I had listed upon my sister-in-law's insistence. I had to write down for her absolutely everything that was on my Wish List. I'd watched enough House Hunters on HGTV to know no one ever gets everything on the Wish List. But I did get it all. Every single thing.

Like other things I was carrying in my bag of secrets, like my upcoming third divorce, my plan to work in Saudi Arabia half the year was not a topic of conversation I initiated when I was with other people. It was no one's business and it involved my finances which were especially no one's business, as we had been fiercely taught growing up. No exceptions. I could head into a few years of official residency in the Lone Star State knowing it was temporary and my work and life in Saudi could most certainly offset any rude or intrusive questions. Sharon and I had already been online researching abayas, the lighter weight covering robe, more like a choir robe than the heavy all covering burqa, and hijabs, the head covering. I would have to wear abayas and hijabs while I was in Saudi Arabia, of course. I'd have to up my game on eye makeup and shoes as was the case for women in Saudi Arabia. In between, if I played my cards right, I could enter this new Wimberley community phase of my life in a limited way with my good daughter story and an exit plan in place. And, I told myself again, I wasn't going to be there much anyway with this new, exciting life. I was so ready.

The six-month road trip during The Year of the Great Shit-storm was coming to a predictable and practical end. I was feeling increasingly vulnerable as my plane landed in Austin in the much-dreaded "new" home state, with no one I knew but my brother and sister-in-law, a few old high school classmates and a couple of college sorority sisters spread across the state. My east coast, academic, professional, consulting, New York Broadway and cabaret worlds were already starting to telescope backwards in my mind's eye. All the parts of myself I had sought out and cultivated and thrilled to over the last forty-three years were peeling away, like heat shields off a recently launched missile. I felt an overwhelming sadness sprinkled with increasing dread. My life was going backwards.

From everything I'd read, the Hill Country, particularly the Austin Area which Wimberley was a part of, was the new hot spot with the coolest vibe. Maybe I could just disappear here. Since starting over was what I was about, maybe this could work. My brother met me at the airport, one of dozens of times he would do that for me over the next few years. His bottom-less cheerfulness and eagerness to help instantly reminded me why he has been my hero my whole life. Even in the days and years we didn't see each other I always knew he was there at a moment's notice. He would repeatedly prove how true that still was during the next few years.

I reached down deep and grabbed a big 'ol handful of Texas Grit. I finally had a plan. And you know what they say about plans. Or at least what God says. Is that thunder I hear? Or a big belly laugh. Worse. What I feared all along when the Texas caper was hatched, I saw His Nib's face, smirking, and I heard him say to me under his breath, "Texas. Really?" His highest disdain had always been reserved for Texas. When all my cowboy boots had finally arrived in our first home together in Connecticut he'd laughed and said, "Well, I guess it's true. You can take the girl out of Texas but not Texas out of the girl." It did not sound like a loving observation. Seems that in my case you can't even get the girl out of Texas. I was right back where I'd started. Would it ever feel like home, even temporarily? It was only temporary, right?

I pulled out the key to my new house, put it in the lock, and turned it. The door opened. I was standing in a long hallway with a white tile floor that took me to the living room over-looking large old live oak trees, their massive sweeping limbs taking my eye out onto a beautiful golf course. Instead of an empty room waiting to be furnished with furniture I mostly didn't have anymore, the room had a lovely sofa of camel colored brushed cotton upholstery with some complementary throw pillows. There was an armchair. On the walls were beautifully framed posters. On the improvised coffee table were candles and some magazines. Moving into the master suite off the living room was a queen-sized bed with a thick Pottery Barn bedspread, coverlet, and pillow shams, a bedside table with a reading lamp. It went on like this throughout the home. The kitchen was stocked with pots and pans, plates, glasses, and cutlery, utensils, a coffee pot and fresh ground coffee in a canister. In the refrigerator were fresh fruit, a simple packaged meal of salmon and asparagus, English muffins, butter, bottled water, a quart of milk, and a bottle of wine. The bathrooms had soft towels on the racks. The large covered back porch had a new wooden glider, a gift from the four of them. Mike and my sister-in law and their next door neighbors, who I'd spent time with over the years, had worked tirelessly in my absence to turn a completely empty space into a welcoming home. There were countless details in every room that warmed the spaces with love and practicality. Boy, did I cry.

At the end of the initial tour my sister-in-law sat with me on the living room sofa and handed me a copy of the wish list email I'd sent her. Beside each item was a blue check mark:

- A Texas limestone façade
- Small or no yard with low maintenance
- Texas live oak trees
- Covered porch
- Wood Burning fireplace
- Separate dining room
- 2 bedrooms/1 ½ to 2 bathrooms (I have three bedrooms/2 baths)
- A view, however small

Who has a family like this? I would live my two years in Texas in style and comfort and with love.

Six weeks later, passports and visas in hand, two days before my team and I were supposed to board a plane for our first trip to Saudi Arabia, the phone rang. It was Jim, the head of the Saudi project. "I'm sorry," he said. "The Saudi project is off."

What Am I Doing In Texas?

Lyrics and Music by Chick Morgan © 2015

What am I doing in Texas?
I ask myself time and again
I swore this was the last place I'd ever step foot in
It just wasn't meant to be a part of the plan.

So, tell me. What am I doing in Texas?
How did I ever get here?
I swore I'd wiped the **** off my red boots forever
Now I'm dancing with cowboys drinking Shiner Bock beer.

Oh, Lordy, what am I doing in Texas?
Did I take a wrong turn somewhere?
I never said I wanted a Luckenbach lover,
Now I'm tricked out in turquoise and I'm growin' big hair

Please help me, what am I doing in Texas?
My friends tell me I won't last long.
But I'm tasting the wine and I'm feeling just fine,
And I'm suddenly writing down this Texas love song.

Please tell me, What am I doing in Texas?
Why did I ever come back again?
Must have heard the Lone Star call of Slaid Cleaves
    and Gruene Hall
And that's what I'm doing in Texas! Yee Haw!

11 – Saying Goodbye To Sondheim

Just keep moving on.
Anything you do let it come from you
Then it will be new.

Lyrics from "Move On,"
by Stephen Sondheim from the musical
Sunday in the Park with George

I never wanted to come to Texas or Wimberley. Everyone else I know in Wimberley made a personal vow or a pinky swear or a Brownie Scout pledge that they would return at some point in their life. I had outgrown Texas personally, politically, spiritually, culturally, and every other way. When asked the inevitable "How did you get to Wimberley?" question, I responded with my well-polished and soon to be well-worn answer: "My mother died, my daddy in San Antonio needed me, and I wanted to be here for him as long as he still recognized me with his rapidly increasing dementia." End of story. Tight story. I told that story so often and it was so tight I actually believed it myself for a while. It prompted the right balance of pity and admiration. Years later, I realized there was a big piece of the story missing.

I knew that moving back to Texas was the best – the right – thing to do. No one needed to know I cringed at the thought of any long term plan to stay here. In my mind that wasn't happening. I did feel a certain amount of righteous self-respect for stepping up to the occasion when it was called for, even if my heart was determined to be on either coast and never dead center in the middle of the country. I really didn't know what I was getting into, but I am a good and devoted daughter. I was determined to make it work—for Daddy. For my brother and sister-in-law. I was also angry to the point of stupefaction when I moved here, simmering with rage at all that I'd given up because of my husband's abrupt and heartless decision to dump me at age sixty-four. My life had been sailing along. Damn you.

My east and west coast friends were aghast that I was thinking about moving here, even for a short time. "How can you stand the politics?" wailed one New York colleague while we stood on the corner of 46th and Broadway hailing a cab after a cabaret performance class. "All those guns!" decried another while we rummaged through Hermes scarves at Bloomingdale's. "How will you survive such a small town and the small minds that go along with it?" munched one over corn beef sandwiches in a deli in Westport. "You won't find a decent bagel or any good tofu," one friend whispered during downward dog at our weekly yoga class. "What will you do about that?" I didn't know. I also didn't know if anyone in Texas had ever heard of Stephen Sondheim, the genius Broadway musical lyricist and composer. How was I going to survive *that*? How was I going to survive living in a place where there was no non-stop flight to Paris from the local airport so I could be there within twelve hours on a whim? How was I going to survive the sneers, looks of bewildered pity, or outright hostility when I told people where I lived? It's only for a short while, I kept telling myself. I was embarrassed to tell people I was moving to Texas at all. It wasn't how I thought of myself anymore and didn't want anyone else to think of me like that either.

Without question, my cabaret days would be over. No more taking the train from Westport, Connecticut at 8:00 a.m. on Saturday mornings and riding for an hour to arrive at the awe-inspiring Grand Central Station, the closest thing New Yorkers have to a public palace, the station much quieter than on a weekday morning or evening, but still baroque and beautiful and busy. In all my years working, playing, and singing in New York, I never tired of walking past the large clock in the center of the station, or going up or down the marble staircases, or enjoying oysters and wildly overpriced martinis at the Oyster Bar. No more walking across Manhattan from Grand Central Station to 46th and Broadway, known as Restaurant Row, where the legendary club Don't Tell Mama was situated in the middle of the block with its piano key awning and stairs down to the bar, or stopping at Starbucks in the Midtown Hilton for my large strong black coffee that would see me through the three hour class, waiting in line behind tourists in thick tennis shoes and space consuming puffy coats. No more intense classes with my eight other classmates in the Saturday Advanced Performance Workshop, my director Lina and musical director Rick, trying out new numbers and arrangements on the stage of Don't Tell Mama. At that early hour on a Saturday morning the club was still napkin strewn and beery from the late night before and in winter, really cold. It was heaven, though, on the stage, under the spotlight and behind the microphone, doing the difficult work, the emotional digging work. Peeling the onion. Digging deeply and honestly. No more stopping at TKTS half-price ticket booth at 44th and Broadway, or walking back to Grand Central to see what tickets might be available for that day's Broadway and Off-Broadway matinees and evening performances. My ritual was to stand there and look at the boards displaying the shows with available tickets and the ever escalating ticket prices even at half price. I would take in the boards and which shows were available that day for matinees, watching them flip over every minute or so like destinations on an airport departures and arrivals board. I'd evaluate the lines and decide if there was anything interesting and whether or not to go.

Don't Tell Mama was just a couple blocks from TKTS, the half-price ticket booth, which is in the heart of the theater district. Our class was over at 1:00. I could make any 2:00 matinee show that had available tickets, and often did. I loved the spontaneity of it. No planning months in advance to get tickets, take a flight from Yodelsville or someplace, find a cheap hotel which doesn't exist, of course. Even the lower end hotel chains which should be affordable are still outrageously high. I didn't have to resort to Hard Rock Café or Burger King. I knew where the old Frankie and Johnny's Steakhouse on the second floor of John Barrymore's former townhouse was, or Joe Allens, Lattanzi, or Becco on west 46th, right down the street from Don't Tell Mama. I knew of some non-touristy delis a few blocks off of Broadway with outrageously good pastrami sandwiches. His Nibs never minded when I took in a show. Saturdays had become writing days for him since I was tied up with the cabaret class. By the time I got home, he'd have a delicious beef stew or pot roast wafting through the house and a big glass of my favorite cabernet poured and waiting.

There would be no more getting to the cabaret club on a late afternoon or early evening of performance day, Don't Tell Mama, The Duplex, or best of all, The Metropolitan Room. I'd descend into what was usually a pretty dreadful "green room," on ancient steep and narrow musty stone steps with a tiny dressing room at the bottom. Waiters carrying trays of drinks, appetizers, or entrees for the restaurant next door charged back and forth and up and down the same stairs as well. One so-called dressing room was nothing more than a curtain hung on a clothesline in a corner of the back area of the club, reminiscent of the Clark Gable fixture in *It Happened One Night.* The Metropolitan Room! Oh, the Metropolitan Room dressing room, a true dressing room with a three-way mirror, a sign on the door with an actual star on it, and my name.

However grand or humble the circumstances, I would emerge dressed in a sequined evening gown and earrings that brushed my neck, hair perfect, slipping on at the last minute my four inch heel Bruno Magli black peau de soie evening shoes, listening to the murmur of the crowd at the tables talking to each other and sipping the first of their "two drink minimum," while the lights dimmed, then waiting in the dark to be announced: "Ladies and Gentlemen, Don't Tell Mama/The Metropolitan Room/The Duplex is proud to present: Morgan!" The piano would start up the intro, the crowd, applauding, eagerly anticipating a smart, well designed, entertaining, emotionally stirring, and professionally presented seventy five minute journey which I always gave them. I looked out over the crowd never really seeing past the first three tables because of the spotlights, singing to the back row regardless. Cole Porter, Johnny Mercer, and always…Sondheim. There is absolutely nothing like it. Nothing. In all those years I never experienced one second of stage fright. Adrenalin? Yes. As I stood in the wings I would think, "This is what I've wanted to do. I am prepared for this! I have something to say! Listen to me, world! How lucky, lucky, lucky am I!"

I was also aware that I was usually the oldest person in the room, the class, or the studio with few exceptions. Like almost everything else of substance I've done in life I started later than most but it never deterred me. Age had never felt like anything particular to me after I reached sixteen and got my driver's license. I didn't have my first real corporate career job until I was thirty, long after the twenty somethings right out of their prestigious schools had begun to make their mark chewing their way up the career ladder with their perfect white teeth. I started my PhD at forty-one. Most, not all, of my friends and fellow cabaret colleagues were fifteen to twenty years younger than me and had come out of highly-regarded musical theater programs or were playing Marian the Librarian in *The Music Man* as high school juniors. But I had Grit. Texas Grit. And when I put my mind to something it happens. After a couple years of hard and consistent training in Connecticut I auditioned in New York for the International Cabaret Conference at Yale, which held auditions all over the U.S. and in London, Berlin, and Sydney. "I'll do it for the audition experience," I told myself. "It will be a good experience."

I worked for a couple months with my local vocal coach in Connecticut getting a few numbers ready. I was told to have a ballad and an upbeat/comedy number. My friend Bert, a former world-class musical director and symphony composer, had put Eartha Kitt's world-wide comeback show together and directed it for several years. Orson Wells once described Eartha Kitt as "the most exciting woman in the world." Her blazing star of fame abruptly flamed out after she made anti-Vietnam war statements at a White House luncheon and was shunned in the entertainment world for almost ten years. Bert finally burned out, too, after many years in the big-stage music business working with major names around the world. His Nibs and I met him as an airport driver and during various conversations we had during tedious waits for luggage arrival in La Guardia, JFK, or Newark, we began to get to know him.

One day, watching the luggage carousel make its tenth rotation and still no bag of mine in view, I turned to Bert and asked, "Is there any chance you would create a special arrangement for me to sing during my Yale audition? I feel I've got to give them something memorable since I'm really a nobody in this sphere." Bert, ever affable and by now a friend responded, "Sure. When do you want to start?" The bag finally appeared, along with my usual bagasm at its long overdue approach.

I told him I wanted an arrangement of Jimmy Webb's "Is There Love After You" and "something else to work into it" which is quite common in cabaret shows, to mash up, I guess you'd call it, two songs that together tell a new story. And here is the genius of a true professional, someone beyond the "good piano player" (often good enough), and light years beyond what a professional musician friend of mine called "the long list of hymn pounders" I had to work with in Texas.

"Let's try this," Bert suggested as he began to softly play the beautiful Stevie Wonder song "All Is Fair in Love." As the music flowed through his fingers and the transitions and modulations wove their magic, I knew we had something special. Bert was old school when it came to music notation. He only composed on full size composition sheets, by hand, in pencil. Every note, every chord, every notation. Even if I couldn't read a single note of music, which I could by the way, thanks to all my years of choir singing, it was a thing of beauty.

The Saturday morning of my audition day, the last of three full days in the New York audition schedule, was crisply cold. The sky was clear and electric blue. Everything I touched or touched me had a spark of static. I put on my street clothes to ride the train into Grand Central. The entire hour of the train ride I was running lyrics in my head or singing softly under my breath the two numbers I was going to sing. The second upbeat number was a little known Cole Porter song called "The Physician " which my local vocal coach in Connecticut, Tom, and I had worked up. We thought it was clever and sassy. I arrived at Grand Central and then walked the few blocks on 45th Street to The Roosevelt Hotel where I usually changed clothes and freshen makeup.

My hair looked good. I am blessed with great hair (thanks,
mom) that was not particularly disturbed even when blown
about by a pretty fierce wind which was blowing that morning.
Just a couple of hand fluffs while I bent over and it was
practically good as new. The outfit I'd chosen was a pair of
classy, flowy navy pants and a red long sleeved V-neck silk
blouse, set off with memorable, dangling silver earrings. I put
on fresh make up and began to make my way to the midtown
address.

I had never been to a New York audition building. It was ten
floors high and each floor's hallway spun off left and right from
the elevator into rehearsal rooms. I headed to the seventh floor.
As the elevator stopped on each floor I could hear classical
piano, Broadway tunes, Caribbean steel drums, tap dancing, and
singers warming up vocally. Someone somewhere in the distance was yelling: "Five! Six! Seven! Eight!" In the opened
doors I could watch dancers attempt body contorting
movements to music.

The elevator stopped on the seventh floor. When I emerged I
saw a three-foot bare wooden bench with a sign above it on
white paper: "Yale Cabaret Auditions – Wait Here" was written
in thick black magic marker. I did what I was told and sat down,
looking up and down the hall, taking in the sounds and sights. A
minute later a woman clutching a clipboard emerged from a
door to the right of the elevator.

"Morgan?" she asked. "Yes!" "Wait here. You'll be called in a
few minutes." She turned and went back into the room. What?
No, "Hi! So glad you could make it. Can't wait to hear you and
good luck?" I could hear through the wall a young man's clear
baritone singing "Nothing's Going to Harm You," one of my
favorite Sondheim songs from the musical *Sweeney Todd*.

The woman with the clipboard opened the door again and brought me to an inner studio room. As I followed her I could feel my beautiful flowy pants working their way right into my butt crack, what with all the dryness and static cling. I thought about trying to discreetly disengage it, but I missed my window of opportunity. I removed my coat and threw it on the indicated chair, making sure I was facing forward and not exposing my ever more uncomfortable backside with the sucked-in fabric.

The room was empty except for an upright piano with an accompanist sitting at the bench, three bare six foot Costco folding tables set in a U-shape, and 7 men, none of whom I'd ever seen before. They, at least, said good morning. They asked for my headshot and bio which I'd learned needed to be on the back of the head shot. I'd had some professional shots taken just for the audition, and the one I chose was really good. In hindsight I realize what an obviously amateur bio I'd written – written to charm, not necessarily to inform. Bad choice. I felt like the inexperienced rube I was. Some months later I heard the derogatory term from one of the Music Directors talking to another Music Director about someone they were working with, "Yeah. Another Fairfield County housewife." I lived in Fairfield County, too. It was a very upscale part of Connecticut and even though I was not a traditional housewife, I got the diss immediately. Is that how they thought of me? Did I come across as a privileged white woman amusing herself as a cabaret singer? Did I feel that way?

Someone introduced the accompanist as Tex Arnold, one of the legendary music directors/accompanists, a very small club. Tex had been the musical director for my good friend whose cabaret show at Danny's Skylight Lounge I'd seen several years before who had inspired me to begin this journey. He had also been the Musical Director for the hit Broadway show *Best Little*

Whorehouse in Texas, with his lyricist friend Carol Hall, another Texan.

"Oh, hello, Tex," I said. "You were the musical director for my good friend Rhonda." Rhonda is memorable for many reasons, most of them flamboyant.

"Oh, yes! Rhonda," he responded. "She was wonderful to work with. How is she?" I replied briefly. I also played my Texas card quickly ("I grew up there!") and handed him the handwritten scores for my two numbers. Tex sat for a few seconds and without looking up breathed, "Oh, these are just beautiful!" Score one for the Fairfield County not-quite housewife. I'd shown them I knew a little bit of how this business worked, how to be a professional. The rest is a blur. I was in and out in ten minutes, back on the train in half an hour, and on my way home to Connecticut.

Thirty-five singers were selected for that year's class, after all the auditions worldwide, and I was number thirty-six on the list. My one page letter in the "thin envelope" stated I was number one on the waitlist and would be notified if there was an opening. I was stunned to even be that close and thrilled with my audition! It was, just as I'd hoped, a great learning experience.

A week later my phone rang. "This is Wendy Lane Bailey from the International Cabaret Conference at Yale. Someone had to drop out. Would you like the spot?" Hell, yes! I made the team! Later I figured out I was the oldest person in the entire class, but so what? It didn't make any difference to me sitting on top of the piano singing my Cole Porter song the night of the Curtain Call performances in the New Theater at Yale several months later. But, I was aware.

I fought hard for my place on the New York cabaret stage and for my place in that world, and thinking I was giving it up because one man was through with me was a tough one to take on the chin. It was one more time I'd been told I was too old to do what I was doing. In one weekend "Summer in the City" intensive in New York, Laurel Masse, a jazz singer best known for her years in the group The Manhattan Transfer, told me when coaching me on a song I'd performed for critique, "You'd better get this right pretty fast, Honey. You're no spring chicken." As if I didn't know.

Leaving New York and Connecticut meant no more opening nights with vases of flowers in the dressing rooms, just like in the black and white movies of the '40's. After the show I would often swoop up an armful of flowers while I met my audience in the bar in cabaret's version of a receiving line. Sometimes I would walk down Restaurant Row with friends, still in my evening gown, on my way to a famous restaurant where another group of friends waited for me, standing and cheering when the maître 'd brought me to the table, regular diners whispering to each other, "Who is that? Who is she?"

In a matter of days after my final New York City show at the glorious Metropolitan Room, almost a year after the Day of Double Heartbreak and the launch of The Great Shitstorm, I was driving from Connecticut to Texas. The cute little Hyundai Sonata (I loved the musical reference) had replaced my down and out VW wagon a year prior. When I took the Sonata out for a test drive with my husband the day I was shopping for a new car he'd asked, "How does it feel?" I was already doing my low, throaty hum, something good cars, good chocolate, good movies, and good sex elicit, and said, "Like I want to go on a road trip!"

I got the road trip. How was I to know I would be driving from Connecticut to Texas a year later – alone. Well, not entirely alone. Frank Sinatra, Johnny Mercer, Cole Porter, Jimmy Webb, Stevie Wonder and yes, Stephen Sondheim, were with me all along the way.

Is all in love fair? Is there love after you? I was going to find out.

Jazz Poem

By Robert O'Meally

Make music with your life
A jagged silver tune cuts every deepday madness
Into jewels
That you wear

Carry 16 bars of old blues with you
Everywhere you go
Walk thru azure sadness
Howlin' like a guitar player

12 – A Little Piece Of Heaven

We're part of all this. We left it, but we can never lose what it has given to us.

> ~ Carrie Watts to her son Ludie
> in Horton Foote's 1985 Film, *Trip to Bountiful*

The locals call it "A Little Piece of Heaven." I wasn't so sure. I arrived in Wimberly, open-minded and willing enough to make my own decision, but not quite convinced. I rolled into that quaint village the first week in September, nine months from the single day of that Double Barreled Heartbreak of my mother's death and the definitive mic drop on my marriage. My third marriage. It was the all too familiar territory of starting over, but this time I didn't have quite the youthful nimbleness, physical or psychological, of my first two do-overs. What could I possibly accomplish in this little not-quite-backwater, sweet Texas Hill Country town that could keep me occupied until my time here with Daddy was done. I thought I had the Saudi project in my back pocket. That wasn't happening now. The initial sting of events earlier in the year had begun to subside some. My travels had been healing, providing an abundance of time for thought, reflection, and looking forward. I still hated the very idea of Texas, but maybe I could carve out a little space here that could work until the next "next step" materialized.

It looked pleasant enough, and, actually, more than pleasant – quaint to the point of having been delivered right out of central casting for a picturesque Texas town, complete with town characters, town rumors, and an interesting old west history. It was also quite the going concern made up with a heartbeat of artists and musicians of every stripe. Original old limestone buildings housed a couple stores, small galleries, a few eateries, all of the buildings hiding a history of whatever they were before – grain stores, a gas station, a small church or two. In no way did this little town look run down and beat up, but curiously, at the same time, it did not seem trendy or trying too hard to be cute and authentic. I would learn over the next few years that singer songwriters and musicians of state and national renown lived quietly in the hills, never far from the Town Square. Some summer mornings I would find one of them sitting quietly with their coffee, reading the Wimberley View in the Wimberley Cafe, minding their own business and others minding theirs as well, sometimes having just dropped their children off at school.

Newcomers to Wimberley and even some old timers describe the town as "magical." I would say it's magical, yes, and more importantly, mystical. There are some good reasons to think so.

The place on this planet I feel most connected to emotionally and spiritually is Ireland. The sacred wells and caves, the stone cliffs and stone landscapes like The Burren in the west of Ireland in County Clare—the music, the gentle hills. Ireland's similarity with the Hill Country has struck me more than once on my dozens of trips there. The Hill Country has its own sacred caves and wells, the result of the underground karst limestone structure with its porous rock that runs underneath the hills—notably in Wimberley's Jacob's Well. The well is famous for its depth and clarity. Its opening is small and it is notorious for being dangerous. Daredevils come from all over the state and even further to take the long plunge into the deep well, navigating expertly through the treacherous opening. The well leads into underground streams and caves and the danger is real and thrilling to those who like that sort of thing.

There is a large granite plateau between Wimberley and Austin. The bold, bald stone expanse is known as Enchanted Rock, an echo of Ireland's Burren region. Some say the magic and mysticism are a result of being on the same ley lines as the Egyptian Pyramids and Stonehenge. Magic? Perhaps. Mysticism? Definitely. A "Little Piece of Heaven?" Most probably.

Once my irritation and disbelief at having to spend time here had subsided, I began to remember how beautiful the landscape is. The outlying acres of vineyards outside of town provide a gentle beauty and accent to the hills. The live oak trees I remembered from my Trinity Baptist Church summer camp days in Comfort, not too far away, spread wide gentle arms across open fields sometimes dotted with cattle and horses, always with deer.

The convergence of two streams of water, Cypress Creek and the Blanco River, water that runs through the town sheltered by ancient cypress trees bending over and shading the waders and floaters enjoying the shallow easy flow during warm, sunny months, is one of the unique charms of Wimberley.

One of the things I hear the most when people move here, after their "How I Got to Wimberley" story, is how at home they felt the first time they ever spent time here, whether they were an eight year old camper or visiting friends who moved here in retirement. Though I still struggle with it years later, a growing part of my heart feels at home here too. I feel joy, feel contentment, feel a kind of opportunity to grow and just *be*, more than any other place I've ever lived. I struggle with it because I still don't want to be seen as a "Texan" and all the political and cultural baggage that goes along with it in my eyes.

But I am willing to be seen as a Wimberley, Texan. That. That is different.

I had been to Wimberley a few times for quick visits to my brother and sister-in-law on trips to visit my parents in San Antonio, usually at about the half-way mark in a visit when my husband and I just felt the need for a little escape. We could drive up I-35 North and be crossing the bridge over the Blanco River into Wimberley in under an hour. Sometimes when I was visiting my parents by myself, I'd stay overnight with my sister-in-law and I would enjoy some shops, a nice lunch out somewhere, and depending on the time of year maybe a leisurely drive on plentiful back roads to enjoy the wildflowers. I wasn't exactly a total stranger.

Over the years I'd met my brother and sister-in-law's neighbors on either side of their home and at an occasional Christmas party, an annual community event which collected toys for the Christmas toy drive for local children. I met a few others, but not many, and not often enough to count any of them as friends. The September I arrived I began to meet people, originally through my brother and sister-in-law who were quite active in the arts communities, as well as the Visitor Center of the Chamber. I attended a Chamber mixer at a local outdoor restaurant. My bullshit and hidden agenda detector was on high alert, but it stayed quiet throughout the evening. I met shop owners and other small businesspeople, musicians, band members, artists, gallery owners, restaurant owners, yoga instructors, lawyers, and (lots) of real estate agents. Everyone had one thing in common: they all loved Wimberley and living here.

I learned quickly that Wimberley is a town where many people move to in mid-life and post-retirement. Other lives and careers are assumed but they are never the lead in any conversation. "What do you do?" or "What *did* you do?" seldom, if ever, come up. It's never cautioned to newcomers as an impolite question to be avoided, either. It's never mentioned at all. Everyone just knows it's not important what you did before, or who you pretend to be now.

When we arrive, we find our long lost or deeply buried passions, jump in, and begin to live them. Want to pursue gardening? Mention it and someone is happy to tell you about the rigorous Master Gardener certificate program for the Hill Country (in which they are probably already certified and happy to show you the ropes to get you in the loop). Want to sing or dust off that much loved and mostly neglected flute or clarinet? Join the Community Chorus or the Hill Country Community Band. Love dogs? Become a volunteer or board member at WAG – Wimberley Adoption Group. Regretting that you didn't follow your heart's dream into the theater after your impressive star turn as Blanch DuBois or Stanley Kowalski in the Senior Class play? Join the board of the Wimberley Players, or, better yet, audition for a play. Love wine? Get on the town-wide email list for Wimberley Wine Share and once a month bring two bottles of your favorite wine and congregate with 50-100 of your fellow wine lovers and friends at that month's chosen business outdoor location and connect, schmooze, and sip. Want to indulge that longing to paint, make jewelry, or fuse glass? Join the Wimberley Art League or find a class or a gallery and let your heart's desire rip. Not an artist but want to support the arts? Join the Wimberley Valley Arts and Cultural Alliance. It may be years (or never) you'll discover, usually by accident, your fellow jewelry maker, singers, actors, or radio hosts are former NASA scientists or astronauts, retired oil company CEOs, international authors, global engineers, renowned writers, academics, teachers, retired professional athletes, even

Superbowl champions. You'll note it briefly to yourself, probably not mention it, and move on. You see, no one really cares who you *were*. We just want to enjoy who you are now and what you can give to this community and each other. Everyone brings their A-Game for this stage of life. It also usually keeps the lid on what will eventually reveal stark political differences. But, for the most part, for the good of the town and most people's genuine love of the life in the town, it takes second, third or fourth place in priorities for most of the year. In other words, Wimberley provides perfect protective coloration for those of us determined to leave something or someone or a past behind and start over.

It was surprisingly easy to make friends, find something enjoyable to do, find something to explore that's always been a dream or a hope. Of course, the politics were there. Most everyone knew who was who. I could figure out who the members of the Wimberley Republican Women's Club were and who were members of the Wim Dems. On the whole, it didn't seem to matter in the larger scheme of things.

There were fundraisers to plan and produce for the Wimberley Players or the animal groups, Friends of the Library, or the Art League. There was always some music going on somewhere and someone to go with and enjoy it and someone to bring you home if the after-concert festivities got a little too festive. I began to call it The Five Minute Town: You are never more than five minutes away from what you want to do. It is very easy to get together for dinner at someone's home or go out or gather to go to a concert or Friday afternoon happy hour. I began to do it. In those days the tools of my life included a camp chair folded up in the back of my car, a Styrofoam ice chest, and an insulated wine cup. I never knew when I'd come across some music somewhere, or a festival, and could unfold my chair and enjoy a "favorite beverage."

My days were busy with board meetings and most of my evenings with music events, art gallery openings, and Chamber mixers. I eagerly swept into the rhythm of Wimberley. These were interesting, accomplished, professional folks. I bet some were also recreating themselves. I wonder how many.

There was no need for anyone to know that I was just passing through. It wasn't a secret, exactly, like the three marriages and divorce thing, but it didn't need to go on the front page of the Wimberley View either.

When I ended up in Wimberley the Year of the Great Shitstorm and started meeting people and getting involved with everything, honoring my personal commitment to say YES to everything (Community Chorus, Chamber of Commerce, Wimberley Valley Arts and Cultural Alliance, The Unitarian Church, Wimberley Institute of Cultures, performing music with my tongue-in-cheek girls' band, The Cashmere Cowgirls, never missing a Wine Share evening or a Whimsy Girls gathering) the only question ever asked of me was the only sure fire question everyone gets: How did you get to Wimberley? I had lots of opportunities to polish my stock answer. Even I began to believe it.

My mother died and my daddy has increasing dementia and I want to…

The people who got to know me after I moved here learned I lived alone in an adorable little house right in town. I hosted small dinner parties and often had friends over for wine on my back porch overlooking the small golf course and the breathtaking Hill Country sunsets whose sheer soul-engulfing beauty I was unprepared for. For a while the Cashmere Cowgirls would practice on Sunday evenings on the porch with the sounds of two (poorly-played) guitars and a stand-up double base (of equal skill) accompanying female vocal harmonies. We sang Guy Clark's "She Ain't Going Nowhere" before I knew who Guy Clark was. We also sang some of the newly penned Chick Morgan originals. I don't think anyone ever knew I had hit the unholy trifecta of three divorces. I assumed the shame and embarrassment I concealed around that might leak and if people knew, all these Jesus-loving, or simply, just loving, couples that had been high school sweethearts, married right out of college and celebrating twenty- five, thirty, forty-plus, even fifty-year anniversaries, would look at me as a whorish freak, which I guess is how I felt deep down. Serial monogamy, I discovered in my wonky need to research these kinds of things, is not the norm. I never wanted to mention the third strike for fear I would be judged unreliable, incapable of sustaining relationships, lacking in values, or perhaps, (my deepest fear) lacking in value.

To my increasing surprise and growing delight, I began to realize that Wimberley was a town created just for me at my age (or so I believed), and particularly at this over-sixty-newly-single stage of my life. Sure, there were others enjoying this remarkable community, but it had been specifically tailored for me. I could do anything I wanted, be anyone I wanted to be. It was easy to meet people and make friends – couple friends, single and married girlfriends, a growing number of friend/colleagues on the many boards I sat on or went out dancing with at The Buzzard Bar in town where half the town ended up mid-week and weekends, listening to music, having a Shiner Bock, and maybe dancing to a tune or two with the live band on the postage stamp size dance floor.

For the first time in my life since high school I was not involved in a relationship. Every relationship in my life was either an intense love affair or a fade out and overlap into another. The baton, however, was never dropped. I never had to stop and think about how one goes from always being married to suddenly single, not only suddenly single for the first time, but at the age of sixty-four. I felt used up and just used; not bitter, not even angry, mostly "Now what? How do I do this?" I was sixty-four, no biological children (although four lovely daughters of affection – or stepchildren.) Both parents were deceased. I have two brothers, neither of whom has biological children. It was hard to make the time to figure out a new life and at the same time keep fear on every possible level from seeping in like a damp basement. The awareness of being pretty much alone in this world, nobody's daughter, nobody's mother, nobody's wife, but still a sister twice over, began to sink in. And none of us were getting any younger.

Although I was still feeling despised, unwanted, cast-off, and ashamed, there was a part – a growing part – of this new single life I really enjoyed, a truth I felt too ashamed to admit. You'd think my shame would at least have a shelf life or capacity issue by this point. Apparently not.

As the reality of living anonymously and without a past sank in, I started behaving in ways my proper Southern Baptist, do-gooder PhD could never have dreamed up. Dinner parties in that adorable little house on the golf course included some raucous evenings with girlfriends. I smoked my first pot on the covered back porch overlooking the fourth green. Lacking any of the standard paraphernalia but having been gifted the main herbal ingredient, I learned how to smoke from a pipe fashioned out of a Coke can with a nail-punched hole, something many people, apparently, learn at a much younger age.

In a bit of musing on the back porch one Sunday night with the Cashmere Cowgirls, doing our version of "rehearsing" but mostly talking about men, I decided to host a dinner party where the three of us would invite some man we'd met, didn't really know, and were intrigued by.

I knew just who it would be. I'd met the man I was considering, tall, gorgeous, fantastic build, and at least fifteen years younger than me, just a few months earlier, house sitting at a friend's group of cabins, waiting for the AC guy to show up, which he did, much to my eventual delight. In addition to talking up to him in the crawl space in the attic, slipping in new hardware and replacing faulty intake ducts, all the while talking about his fantastic – maybe fantastical? – life and career, we hit it off. Did he really own a wild game ranch in West Texas where he entertained boldface name stars? Had he really been an airline marshal, all gunned up and anonymously boarding planes across the country in the years after 911? I. Did. Not. Care.

I decided that Gorgeous AC Guy would be the one. After completing his work, saying goodbye, and returning to his truck that day we met, I drove by him on my way out just in time to see him remove his surprisingly neat and clean ballcap, no stupid or disgusting slogans embroidered on it, a real plus. A golden waterfall of hair let loose and tumbled all the way to his waist. Yes, this would do.

The planned dinner party turned out to be the same evening two friends from Connecticut were staying with me – impromptu house guests, something I always enjoyed.

I postponed, procrastinated, and chickened out calling my prospective date. He'd given me his card in case I ever had any AC issue. Hey. It's Texas. It's always a real possibility. Over the weeks leading up to the dinner, I repeatedly chastised myself for not only engaging in but initiating such a trashy, or what felt to me as trashy, move. I had never – ever – come close to doing anything like this in my life, but what the heck? I was reinventing myself. I had no handbook, so why not, for the first time in my life, write my own? Only after the other guitar player said she'd invited her guy did the last shred of self-respect (at least towards my friend if not myself) kick in. I called him. After all my upbringing as a good Southern Baptist GA Queen Regent, even after three husbands and divorces, after still managing to squirrel away a modest cache of rubies, I felt mortified asking a man like this to a thing like this: someone I didn't know at all to what clearly looked like an open invitation to who knows what. The conversation went something like this:

"Hi. I met you a couple weeks ago at the cabin when you were fixing the AC and enjoyed talking with you. I'm having a little dinner party on Saturday and wanted to see if you could come." Silence. Oh, my god. He feels cornered and is going to worm his way out somehow. He can't even abide the idea of doing this. Guess he's chortling into the back of his hand while he's driving…which he clearly was, driving, at least. I'm already mortified.

"Uh, yes, I'm pretty sure I can come. Where do you live?"

I told him.

Crickets.

"Who is this again? And where did I meet you?"

So, there it was. After weeks of complete paralysis in calling him because I would be so embarrassed at his embarrassment at my embarrassment, he didn't even remember who I was. Could my embarrassment get any worse? My worst fear was front and center. I felt like a ridiculous old lady trying pathetically not to be, at the same time hitting on a much younger man. I felt a cold chill tinged with embarrassment that my flirtation days were over. Damn. Where was my old life? How on earth did I get here, to this moment? Why wasn't I at one of my favorite restaurants in New York or Connecticut or Santa Barbara with my husband, enjoying a good Pinot Noir and planning our next trip to our Paris apartment? How did I get into *this* mess? What am I doing here?

Surprisingly, Golden Adonis Man said yes. I waited a moment or two for it to sink in. Okay, now test number two: Would he show up?

He did show up, almost on time, wearing a nice western jacket and jeans, his long blond tresses almost contained in a free style ponytail of sorts, a bolo tie, and white cowboy hat, the good kind, as the inside hat band was marked 50X, meaning it had a reasonably high ranking in the quality of the hat itself. With straw hats, the X indicates how tight the weave is and how narrow the straw reed used to make the hat, and since this was straw, that was a good sign. He was holding a bottle of white wine in each hand, one unopened, the other half consumed. *Not* a good sign.

With uncomfortably high energy I said, "Come in! And thanks for the wine!" He handed me the unopened bottle and continued into the living room still carrying the partially consumed one.

Me, nervously again since I don't yet know a lot about cowboy hat protocol, "Should I take your hat?"

"Sure, thanks. Cool house. You live here long?" He walked over to the fireplace where a low-burning early-season fire flamed, next to one of the tall windows on either side looking out over the golf course, which was green and inviting. A golf cart ferrying a dad and a couple of small boys whizzed by. A dog walker leading a teacup Yorkie strolled a path on the golf course. A peaceful evening picture.

The idea for such an evening developed a few months back when my New England girlfriend was visiting. I was whining about no elegant dinner parties in Wimberley – nothing like what we used to throw often in our New York and Connecticut days. We decided to replicate one of those wonderful evenings, and when I discovered my friend Jack was coming the same weekend, it seemed the perfect opportunity.

"A few years," I replied to his question. I now stood in the middle of a perfect portrait of contrasts in my own living room. I was tastefully, even elegantly attired in cashmere and pearls and tailored Max Mara slacks. My two visiting friends from New England, one a prim and elegant English-born and New England raised woman, the other a European man, trained chef and wine connoisseur, and literate in all things New York and the world. The two other Cashmere Cowgirls were in boots and loose, lacy blouses, and in the center of it all, Golden Adonis Cowboy as I would always think of him, which I did often.

The other invited gentleman eventually showed up in bare feet sporting a six-inch braided goatee anchored with a tasteful silver Celtic charm. When he appeared at my door, he was admonished by his Cashmere Cowgirl date to "go back to the truck and please put on shoes, for God's sake. This is a nice party." Without any complaint and with a slightly puzzled look, he went back to his truck and a few minutes later returned wearing Tevas and carrying a half-consumed bottle of white wine, apparently a theme at work here. He was courteous and apologized for being late and barefoot. OMG, I thought. This evening is going to be epic. It was. My two New England guests had offered to plan the menu and do all the cooking and all the serving for which I was most grateful, freeing me up to focus on, well, everything else.

I had set the dining table (in an actual dining room, thank you) with good linens, candleholders and tapers, silver, linen napkins, beautiful serving dishes and utensils, and crystal water and wine glasses. We all stood around the table together before getting seated. Braided Goatee Barefoot Man said, "Wow. This is really nice. I've never seen anything like this before." I was touched.

The drinks flowed, the appetizers and entrée were delicious, the table elegant, and that's about all I remember. Sometime during the evening my date suggested we take a walk on the golf course, ending up on the fourth green. He grabbed me and kissed me like I hadn't been kissed, well, ever.

"Hmmm, Darlin'. If you make love as well as you kiss we're going to have a good time. Come on back with me to the ranch, Sugar." How could I? I had two house guests. A true southerner would never abandon a house guest!

I'm not sure what happened to the rest of the meal while the Cashmere Cowgirl and her Braided Goatee Barefoot Man and I, and Golden Ponytail Adonis, were on the back porch smoking pot.

My two visiting guests had cleaned up the table and the kitchen and apparently gone to bed. The third Cashmere Cowgirl, being the mother of a teenage boy, begged off to go home because, as she usually said, "I have to make sure the house and The Boy are still standing." The next morning my visitors informed me we never got to the last two courses: the salad and dessert, plus, coffee and the after-dinner liqueurs. Dang.

Since turning down his compelling invitation on the 4th green to come back to his ranch, I've only seen him or talked to him two more times, an amazing feat in this small town. The first time a few weeks after the dinner a phone call woke me after midnight and a low, sexy, almost familiar voice said, "Hey, darlin'. I'm missing you. I'm lonely at the Ranch. Can I come over?"

"No," I said, my voice still froggy with sleep, which probably sounded sexy to him – and hung up. I woke up the next morning with a jolt. Oh. My. God. At age 65 I'd received my FIRST BOOTY CALL. Yee Haw! That took a little while to joyously sink in along with a little self-congratulation. Well, Okay. A *lot* of self-congratulation.

The last time I saw him was many months later. I was making an uncharacteristically late-night run at 9:00 p.m. (late for Wimberley) to our revered Texas grocery store, H-E-B, which we are very fortunate to have a smallish branch of here in Wimberley. The store was almost empty. I wheeled my cart around from one aisle to the next and suddenly there he was, leaning in the doorway to the back storage rooms talking to one of the workers.

He didn't see me. I deftly swung up the canned soups and vegetables aisle making the same kind of practiced U-turn I'd perfected over the past year when about to run into someone I didn't have the time to talk to, one of the lovely but often inconvenient social hazards in this small town. I made my skillful, usually effective evasive maneuver. Oops, there he was again. I feigned surprise and struck a casual pose at my basket:

Well, hello there. How are you?

Hey, good to see you. How have you been?

Okay. And you?

Yeah, busy at the exotic wildlife ranch. I hear you have a boyfriend.

Yes. Have for a while now. He's great. I hear you have a girlfriend. And did when I met you.

Sheepish grin and hound dog hung head. "Yeah, I guess I did. Your guy's a lucky guy."

"Well, see you around," I said, scurrying around the corner into the next aisle, hoping our scintillating exchange diverted him enough he hadn't noticed the 48-roll package of toilet paper in my cart. The conversation did not top the "if you make love as well as you kiss, we are going to have a great time" line of our former encounter. Then again, nothing much ever would. I haven't seen him again, although I keep my eyes peeled.

He couldn't be considered Totally Inappropriate even though he was probably fifteen years younger, or more. I had no benchmark anymore to gauge what was appropriate or not. Pretty liberating. Certainly intimidating. I had little experience in a world in which I wasn't playing by rules someone else crafted and measuring up to standards someone else thought were admirable, the ones I'd find if I ever went to Sunday School again or read the Girls Auxiliary Manual again. Were all bets off? Just some? Had the statute of limitations finally run out for the copyright on The Good Girl Manual? Would rubies ever be involved again? In the meantime, yes, I did have a boyfriend and had jettisoned an earlier one as well. Life was good.

The other half of the secret in my new life was this: For the first time in my adult life, I could look around my home and every room, every *thing* in every room, and whatever my eye fell upon, was something that pleased me and I wanted there. No aesthetic compromises. No shelves of hand painted miniature soldiers posed in various battle stances, crafted by West Point Starter Husband, figures so small they must have been painted with an eyelash; no shoe racks of beat up Hush Puppies and frayed jeans and lime green leisure suits, preferred wear of Hyphen-Husband; no cane and metal Breuer dining chairs with the awkward arms that prevented any single one chair fitting underneath the dining table and therefore blocking an additional two feet of space around the entire table – sixteen years of those miserable chairs. I greatly admired the Nambe serving bowl; the Irish woven textile throw tossed over the arm of my sofa; a spectacular large black and white print of a young Frank Sinatra sitting on a rehearsal stool in his white shirt and loosened tie, studying the score of his song with the orchestra taking a break in the background. Yes, I liked those pieces of his very much even *before* I managed to artfully liberate them from our home when I left. I also gave my large, colorful painting of the kissing tango dancers from a gallery in Montmartre the pride of place in the living room it had always deserved but never been "allowed."

I have a friend who had two long, deeply satisfying marriages and was widowed twice. I have another friend who had two marriages and divorces and the third one was her life-love for over a decade, and then she was widowed. I, certainly not to my credit, repeatedly bemoaned the fact that I was always one good insurance policy away from a comfortable old age. That would certainly have softened the financial and psychological blow at this point in my life of three marriages and divorces. But, no.

I've done a lot of thinking about all of this, and frankly, I really don't get it, other than to say I seem to have a lot of qualities, apparently on the surface or on paper or upon just meeting me, that attract men early and strong but don't seem to wear well in the long run. Men seem to like the idea of me more than the me of me. One liked the idea that I was from a military family and seemed to know the ropes but didn't like it when I started straining against those ropes when they began to feel like bondage keeping me from exploring other things in life, like growing an intellect. One liked the idea of my getting a master's degree but only because it would enhance his status and make me a better asset as a wife. Looking back I marvel I never questioned the essential meaning of that word, asset:

> *n. a useful or valuable thing, or quality; property owned by a person or company, regarded as having value and available to meet debts, commitments, or legacies.*

I heard it so often my entire life it was part of my DNA. "You'll be such a great asset to a man someday." Well, I didn't want to be an asset to anyone but myself anymore. I had a brand new opportunity to explore, to try on new artistic endeavors. Sure, I knew I could be and had been a really good New York Cabaret singer, but there was so much more to do – and be. I'd had a great career as a Fortune 500 corporate strategy consultant and business owner, but I decided to check that box and see what else was out there in the world.

Landing in "A Little Piece of Heaven" gave me the perfect opportunity to cast off those old labels of loss and failure. They didn't disappear completely, of course, but they took a back seat to who I was learning I could be. Landing in Wimberley, with all the musicians and songwriters, recording studios, festivals, and music venues, I knew I could write some songs and learn how to play them, too. There was no reason Morgan PhDiva couldn't become The Cowgirl Diva. There was no reason this corporate consultant couldn't use all those operation and organizing skills in service of becoming an Arts Entrepreneur, producing festivals, retreats, and bringing new artistic enterprises to life, my own, and those of organizations in town.

Landing in "A Little Piece of Heaven" would also mean, over the next few years, I would find my personal center of gravity for the first time with friends, creatives, intellectuals, writers – the centerpiece of what I think of today as my true community – the people who get me and support me and challenge me and love me.

"Set your heart on fire," wrote the poet Rumi. "Then surround yourself with people who fan the flames." I have, and I did, right in a Little Piece of Heaven.

A Little Piece of Heaven

Words and Music by Susan Gibson ©2017

They call our town a paradise, the jewel of the Blanco River
Postcards and tee-shirts advertise
"A Little Piece of Heaven"
These trees have stood for centuries with their feet
    in the blue green water
Witnesses to world wars and the christening of generations
    of sons and daughters
Amen. Amen. Amen.

We built our homes out of the rock
And we've always prayed for rain
The faithful and the fragile flock
Would stand another drought again
And as the storm clouds gather and the dust turns into mud
We grab on to each other
Was the only way to survive the flood.
Amen. Amen. Amen.

So many have lost so much, and some have lost it all
And I'm thankful for the safety net
The folks who catch us when we fall
Amen. Amen. Amen.

Those who were left upon the shore to behold
    the cruel ascension
New angels knocking on the door of a little piece of heaven

you see it:

…the extraordinary mass of blond hair bricked up as high as the apprentice hairdresser could reach on her little plastic footstool…the orange canned-tan smashed into a pair of ripped stone-washed designer jeans with silver crosses stitched on the back pockets…and the black silk tour jacket with nothing but JESUS spanning the entire back of it in bright, blaring pearly-white letters…

Nathan Brown from *Just Another Honeymoon in Paris*
© 2019 Mezcalita Press

I'll be honest. I hate the phrase "it's all good." It creeps into every crevice and wormhole of our language. I think I understand a person's intention to reflect optimism, faith, personal peace, and all that, but it seems shallow, like a hand going up on the part of the speaker in a "Stop in the Name of Love" motion to deflect a whole lot of other things. It cuts off any difference of opinion, questioning, permission to express pain or anger or abandonment or heartbreaking loss so enormous that words are impossible and even unnecessary. Maybe that's why it's caught on so widely. It keeps me or you from having to find those specific words, rage against the unfairness, or let rip with ugly crying. I've heard friends utter those words looking down and twisting a Kleenex after being informed their job had been eliminated. They are the sole support for their family, little in savings, and no health insurance. So, what part of *that* All is good? I have heard from another close friend who uses the phrase relentlessly through several years ping-ponging from one devastating health crisis to another, one stumble towards death's door after another, with even more debilitating news. "Don't worry. It's all good." All? Oh, come on.

I've come to believe that the "good" part, if it exists, is only visible long after the actual event. While I am in "it," it is shit and may feel like shit for a very long time. Part of what makes it feel like shit is the sheer ambiguity of shelf life. What makes the difference is recognizing the hand we've been dealt at this moment is shit. Just give me the courtesy of that one moment with you to acknowledge the awfulness, and then maybe, if circumstances warrant, and in the right time, I can think about survival, or even abundance. Over time we will determine if it has evolved into something worthy of the label *good*.

Arriving in Texas to live was not, in the beginning, even re-motely "all good." But a lot of it was better than I'd feared. At first, the sheer shock of my complete immersion back in Texas culture consumed a lot of mental oxygen, including resuming my old first name, a nickname, after forty three years. The pleasant weather was a surprise, along with the infusion of dozens of wineries throughout the Hill Country from Austin to Fredericksburg. The Southwest Texas State Teachers College of my childhood had morphed into the 40,000 plus student Texas State University in San Marcos fifteen miles away. Erratic little heartbeats of hope fluttered to let me know all might not be lost, particularly when I read about the opening of a new Performing Arts Center there.

In spite of these promising signal flags of hope, I often woke in the middle of the night with a feeling of combined dread and embarrassment over the knowledge I actually lived in Texas. All the unfavorable projections and assumptions that the reason-able people I'd known and lived amongst for decades would now be aimed at me as well: parochialism, narrowmindedness, rude meat-eaters, Bible thumping megachurch attenders, and the accents! God help us! After all the months of denial and years of protestations about ever setting foot here again, the evidence was clear. The jabs of reality were too obvious to ignore. How was I going to stand it?

After a few weeks in town I realized survival for the next two years or so was dependent on keeping my mouth shut about The Three Big G's – Grub, God, and Guns. I had been a vegetarian trending towards veganism for over a year and I was now square in the heart of beef land. My well-meaning older brother who'd taken up cooking in a big way upon retirement a year earlier, invited me to dinner in that first year or so about three times a week, invitations I was relieved and grateful to accept. In those early months living in Wimberley I felt fragile emotionally, and he and my sister-in-law lovingly treated me as a little orphaned bird needing some rest, sustenance, and sweet peace for recovery. And I did need those things. And every night I was there I ate beef or chicken, quietly, thankfully.

Shortly after arriving in the Lone Star State I went to visit my younger brother and sister-in-law in Midland, where they have lived for probably 30 years. West Texas is a country unto itself. It's the visual image I used when preparing for the big Saudi project – all sand, tumbleweeds, and lots and lots of oil. It is a classic oil boom and bust economy. As a musician and music producer, my brother Ken's successful recording studio business routinely fluctuated from sky high with never enough time, equipment, or qualified assistants to handle the load of clients, to bottomed out, moving from the most recent great studio space back into his garage. Whatever the state of affairs, he consistently played, gigged, and produced. He has always been the real deal. When I went to visit them after The Great Shit Storm, Midland was booming with housing construction, new fancy pickup trucks everywhere, oil wells pumping on every scrap of land, tent cities blooming on any and every vacant lot, and the infrastructure to support all of it making traffic and prices a nightmare.

The first time I went to visit them they honored me by taking me to dinner at the biggest and best steakhouse in West Texas, insisting I get the supersized whatever. At the time I had not eaten much beef and no steak at all for over a year. I sat across the table from them, the enormous menu covering my entire upper body, fearful that something dramatic would happen when I did eat my inevitable steak, which of course I was going to do, and in some alternate universe, craved. I hadn't thought about red meat or missed it in the least, had never felt deprived with my plant-based whole foods eating regimen. But crossing the state line into Texas where eating steak is a sacred ritual, I felt the first faint stirrings of desire, like spotting an old lover across a room.

The steak arrived. It smelled fantastic. It sizzled with corridors of fat around the edges. I dove into it and the shockingly enormous baked potato nestled beside it, blessed with sour cream, butter, chives, and bacon bits. I took the first bite of each. Somewhere in that giant steak house an angel band burst forth with Leonard Cohen's "Hallelujah." I didn't get sick, but my stomach felt stretched and overloaded for three days. I did return to my primarily plant based regimen for the next few years, however the barrier had been breached, and my daily diet was more and more peppered with Texas chili, a hamburger or two, and ah, yes, blessed steak.

I learned early on I must never use the argument of how meat is bad for the body and the planet without expecting to get shouted down somewhere in the conversation. One of my favorite women friends I'd gotten to know in the religiously liberal Unitarian Universalist church, in nearby San Marcos, lost it with me when I mused out loud that we should probably make vegetarian tacos as well for our church summer picnic on the grounds, and not just beef or chicken, given how committed we were as a religious body to the sanctity of animal life and our commitment to reducing climate change. Or so I thought.

"I have three teenage boys and they have to get their protein, so don't talk to me about giving up meat," this normally cheerful and sweet friend bellowed. I didn't. I didn't mention that there is more nutrient filled protein in plants than meat, but most people have difficulty wrapping their heads around that spinach leaf. To each his own. I stayed quiet when I talked about grub.

The Protestants are everywhere, enthusiastically spearheaded by Team Baptist. Their presence informs a lot of aspects of life, although just like politics, it is seldom, not never, but seldom, the leading topic of conversation. Having been gone from Texas for so many those years I was startled to hear public prayer for civic events, school events, and just about everything else "where two or three are gathered in His or anyone's name." When I tentatively ventured out to tell a few people I was attending a Unitarian Universalist Church in San Marcos fifteen miles away, I'd get questions about "What do Moonies believe anyway? I've always been curious." "What's it like in a cult?" A good friend of mine who moved down here, also from Connecticut, relayed her first encounter in the local grocery store. As she tells it:

"I was wandering through the aisles and stopped in the frozen vegetables and struck up a conversation with the woman standing there next to me who was apparently evaluating the merits of the store brand frozen peas and a national brand. I happened to mention I was new to Wimberley and really liked this local Texas store."

"Oh, how lovely you're here! Welcome to Wimberley!" she drawled, and seemed genuinely happy to meet my friend and welcome her, and then immediately asked, "Have you found a church home yet? I'd be happy to pick you up on Sunday." My friend was taken aback, not quite sure what that meant or how to answer. Like the smell of barbeque, religion is always in the air but doesn't always need to be consumed on the spot. I began to get reacquainted with the fact that it is there at all. When the holidays rolled around at the end of the year I was flabbergasted to hear about Christmas parties and Christmas Bazaars. Really? People still say that?

Guns were another story.

After living so many years just across the New York state border and off and on in The City, guns were mainly a topic of conversation when there were headlines about a mob shootout in Lennie's Oyster House in Brooklyn, or when a street gang went on a shooting spree killing each other as well as innocent children sleeping in their beds. In all the forty-three years outside of Texas I'd never held or even seen an actual pistol, and certainly not an AR-15.

While dating High School Boyfriend Bob, he and I would go to his family ranch on weekends and holidays about ninety miles west of San Antonio. Thanksgiving usually coincided with deer hunting season, shotgun season that is, as there is also black powder season in some parts of the country, and bow and arrow season. Someone once tried to convince me there was a "strangling season," where you sneak up on the deer and strangle them. I sputtered outrage at the practice and my usual good girl be nice persona got shot to hell, so to speak. I let that person have it with a torrent of the most judgmental words I could think of, until I realized I was being made a fool. Not new territory. It turns out there is no such thing as strangling season, but it sure sounded plausible to me at the time.

The few times we'd gone hunting before, my boyfriend and I got up pre-dawn and hiked to the deer blind out in the middle of nowhere at the edge of an oat pasture. I was never sure it was called a blind because the deer couldn't see us in the small square wooden box on stilts and small peep holes, or because unless I or he was actually looking out of the peepholes there was absolutely nothing to see. The theory of the case was that the deer would come to the pasture for the oats and kablooey! Let 'em have it. Usually, because we'd gotten up so early, by late in the afternoon I'd be freezing in the heaterless deer blind, still wearing my giant Minute Maid orange juice can "rollers" under a large headscarf, seeing nothing and completely uninterested if I *had* seen anything. But love is love, right?

On this day it was turning nearly dusk, and the law states you can't shoot after dusk. I was getting my gear together in anticipation of finally getting out of the tight wooden contraption on stilts when High School Boyfriend Bob said, "Shhh…look…way out there at the edge of the pasture…this is probably the only shot you'll get today, so why don't you give it a try. It's a nice little buck." I could see absolutely nothing from where I sat. I took the rifle (which should never have happened in anyone's sane world), carefully lifted it to my shoulder and looked through the scope. Wow. The buck was a very long way away, just a tiny dot on the edge of the pasture, even looking through the scope. I take gun safety seriously and have been taught some hunting protocols. I knew the exact spot between the neck and shoulder I should aim for. Today, I hate that I know this.

I know at this point in the saga purists have already tuned me out and dismissed anything that's coming next because I had a scope, very controversial and considered to be cheating by some hunters. I took my one shot and felled what turned out to be a nine point buck at about 300 yards. I was still pretty ho-hum about the whole thing, glad it was over with and we could go back to the house for one of his mother's great chicken fried steak, fried okra, and mashed potato and gravy dinners.

The shot turned out to be a big deal to some others, though. High School Boy Friend Bob marked off the distance between the deer blind and the dead (thank goodness) buck, and that's how he came up with the 300 yards. Not exactly a precise metric. On the drive back to San Antonio we stopped for gas and High School Boyfriend Bob got a lot of congrats and slaps on the back from the guy putting the gas in the car and a couple of other hunters who had pulled over, until he corrected them, rather proudly, I have to admit, that the buck was mine. Then the whoops and hollers really started. It would have been fun, I guess, if I were into that kind of thing, but I really didn't care. I would have been fine just passing the (credit for) the buck... even when my buck was dressed out in pounds of venison steaks, chops, and hamburgers. I don't even like venison. The shot made the papers, I guess because I was just a high school girl in hair rollers. High School Boy Friend Bob talked me into mounting the rack (antlers), which was a pretty pathetic sight. Nine points sounds impressive, but the set of antlers spanned about nine inches. Why I kept that threadbare shaggy skull for so many years I still don't know. Maybe it proved something to me like it proved to so many testosterone infused boys and men, but if so, what? I was uncomfortable contemplating what my answer might be.

Years later I think about that afternoon and am sickened at the carnage. I do understand in parts of the country it is a rite of passage and ritual handed down from parents to children. I do understand that there are instances where that much detested (in my estimation) venison is indeed eaten to supplement other food, or simply because it is enjoyed. In the many intervening years since that afternoon I have lived in places where deer are considered a nuisance for destroying serious and not so serious gardens. I have personally spent many hundreds of dollars on beautiful garden plants that didn't survive a season or even an overnight in my garden. I didn't know that Hosta is considered the salad course. In the midst of my agitation at them, it would never occur to me or anyone else I knew in my New England and New York worlds to actually *kill* them with a rifle. Some neighbors in my neighborhood, known for its competitive gardening, advocated poisoning them, which disgusted me as well. One particularly energized cohort wanted to sterilize them by feeding them a certain kind of deer chow, which triggered loud emotional outbursts for reasons I still don't get. Would they really rather poison them? But shoot them? Nobody I knew even owned a gun.

Even years after leaving Texas with West Point Starter Husband, who must have had great facility with guns of all kinds being a West Point graduate and commissioned in the Infantry, guns were never part of my day to day life. Starter Husband had to have been extremely familiar with them, but it was never part of his persona as a man. It was a tool to inter-vene in a situation between life and death, not blowing the heads off of game. In full transparency, I did shoot a charging javelina at my boyfriend's ranch, executing a perfect drop and shoot maneuver to one knee, just like in *Out of Africa.* But that one was a real necessity. If only Robert Redford had been there to wash my hair.

Guns were not fashion accessories or household items in my social and professional circles. We would much rather have sliced someone down to size with a well-executed and nuanced metaphor or an elusive and impressive literary reference. The whole shooting-the-buck episode became a humorous bit I used to entertain my corporate colleagues, as it played against type for me.

"It was horrific! It was awful! There I was in Minute Maid juice can hair rollers shooting a buck!" I even included a humor song by social satirist songwriter Cheryl Wheeler in one of my cabaret shows, *Don't Forget the Guns!* It was performed with a rousing Western hoedown style tune and a lot of camp, and it was always a Vaudvillianesque hit. One of the reasons it came across as funny in a New York cabaret show was precisely because it was so outrageous, so extreme in the worlds we inhabited.

Now let's get the kids and pack up the car
Take that vacation we've been waiting for
Drive across this country leave our worries far behind
Singin' four-part harmony to "Sweet Adeline."
'Cause I've got these books and maps from Triple A
We'll visit friends and sites along the way
So, bring the bikes and toys and diapers, pay the neighbor's son
And call to stop the mail and, honey, Don't forget the guns.
Now don't forget the guns you know exactly what I mean
Bring the pistols, bring the Uzi and the old AR-15
We don't look for trouble, but by golly if we're in it
It's nice to know we're free to blow nine hundred rounds a minute.[12]

Those were the days before the perpetual mass school shootings, mall massacres, dance club automatic weapon spraying, targeted Walmart shootings, and some semblance of shared proprietary norms, or at least the norms I was familiar with "back east" in my liberal blue state bubble. Living twenty miles from Sandy Hook Elementary School, even we had to come face to face with what guns in the wrong hand and wrong place did.

Years later when I returned to Texas and became a singer-songwriter myself, I worked on a satire song called "I'm Sassy Sweet and Packin' Heat." The phrase came straight off a bright pink business card I'd retrieved off a bulletin board outside of a ladies room in a tacky taco-dive near Dallas. "Armed Amigas. We're Sassy Sweet and Packing Heat." From a structural and campy point of view my song was really getting somewhere, but over time I could never finish it. What started out as a sassy satire and identified as "one of those Chick Morgan songs that you know you are in for a good time," became a graceless ham-fisted attempt to give air and light to a growing list of cultural tragedies with each year, with each child felled in their ele-mentary desk seat, with each Wednesday afternoon Walmart shopper looking for the mid-week special and ending up in the wrong aisle out of sheer bad luck. None of that was "good."

My real education about guns came early in my transition to Texas.

Wimberley Market Days have been a social and commercial institution in Wimberley since 1964 when the first market was held in the town square. Local vendors set up for business on the tailgates on their trucks, selling everything from pigs, rugs, homemade tamales, and just about anything else you can think of and make a buck from. Most items sold for $10 or less.

Today the market, now the second largest in the state, sprawls over twenty oak-tree-shaded acres with over 475 booths. There is live music set up around the market in multiple locations, usually a lone singer-songwriter singing some originals or good covers, playing Texas swing like Bob Wills, or classic George Strait two-step. There are half a dozen food booths selling barbeque so that the music wafts throughout the grounds mixed with that distinctive wood smoke aroma I can smell 20 yards away from the Pavilion with dozens of food workers and the picnic tables and slab dance floor, all the way to the Lions Club Hamburger Haven up a hill overlooking the alleyways and paths of the market. It's the kind of experience that everyone agrees is a fun event that does good for a lot of people and organizations in town. It's one of the many events, maybe the biggest in Wimberley, that keeps us focused on the good that gets done, maybe one of the few things that really IS all good.

Locals come regularly and keep a list on their refrigerators throughout the year with reminders of whose booth to visit for specific items. Others come from across the state and the region. The traffic in town is "murder" on Market Days and we love it. The bumper to bumper traffic begins four miles away at The Junction where Ranch Road 12, the direct and only route from San Marcos and I-35, intersects with Farm To Market Road 32, bringing the folks in from the west and the north, Blanco, Fredericksburg, Austin. The locals know to get there at 7:00 a.m. and to be honest, for those of us who have fought or continue to fight the day to day traffic in Austin and Houston or Dallas or even New York, it's really nothing. Market Days are great for the town and the high energy and happy vibe is palpable. The $10 price point is long gone and now, in addition to silverwork, vintage and trendy clothes, paintings and sculptures by local artists, you can also find handmade high-end custom furniture selling in the hundreds and even thousands of dollars. Locals also know to come early to snag the primo parking spots closest to the gates allowing them to easily wheel their red wagons and trolley carts, empty now but hopefully filled to the brim when they leave early afternoon.

It costs five dollars to park in the Lions Field across from the Market gates, but no one cares. In fact, you can actually feel good about spending the money and handing it over to the yellow-aproned attendants who unfailingly greet you with a very cheery, "Good morning! Beautiful day for Market Days!" even if it's cold, overcast, or rainy. It always feels like a good day for Market Days.

The money from the market fixtures and rentals, food vendors, and parking all goes back to the Lions Club, which distributes tens of thousands of dollars back into the community every year in contributions to other nonprofits in Wimberley and some substantial high profile scholarships to students of the two local high schools. This cycle of nonprofits generating events to generate big dollars that go right back into the nonprofits of the community is the true economic fuel of this community. There is no way I can feel bad about spending any money. I always run into many friends, both among the 200 plus volunteers who staff everything from parking to directions to food booths, to neighbors just moseying the aisles and winding paths. Any nonprofit organization can send volunteers to work at Market Days and in return their organization gets their hours noted and receives contributions back at the end of the year, the most worthwhile and innovative structure for organizational kickbacks I've ever experienced. In our impromptu run-ins we chat about recent board meetings, who's running for City Council, who's got something new and fabulous at their regular booth, where did the beautiful plants I'm eyeing in your cart come from, and everything else neighbors talk about on a beautiful, sunny, summer or fall morning.

I've scored some classic finds. My first sort of adult guitar, spotted by my eagle-eyed sister-in-law, bright red enamel and at a doable one hundred dollars, was one of my first market acquisitions. Among others were handmade soaps, pottery, jewelry, sundresses, and wrought iron lawn ornaments. However, nothing prepared me for my stroll by a booth on the second or third Market Days I attended.

From twenty feet away the booth looked like a typical booth, about 20 feet deep, 20 feet wide, gray barnwood siding not in particularly good or bad shape, a metal roof, merchandise visible inside as well as on metal hang bars in front outside. The soft, hand sewn quilted shoulder purses in cute, colorful Laura Ashley and Liberty of London fabrics caught my eye. I picked up one of the bags and slung it on my shoulder, fingering the fabric to get its feel. It was well made. I looked past the purses on the rods and saw an entire booth filled with purses and bags – different sizes, different patterns, different colors. The booth drew a group of ten or twelve women both inside and on the porch doing the same kind of admiring and fondling. And then I saw it.

A discreet laminated yellow sign just off to the side on the right side of the building next to the door, about 8"x 10" proclaimed: Ask Us About Our Concealed Carry[13] Bags. "Oh, this is fabulous!" I thought. "I can't wait to send a picture of this to my friends in New York and Connecticut. They will never believe this! What a hoot!" I was already composing the snarky email in my head dissing Texas as I took out my phone, something along the lines of "See? What'd I tell you? I wasn't kidding!" While I was snapping another photo, a woman walked up to me. She was about five feet tall wearing a jumper made out of very similar material to the purses. On her sturdy looking feet were black, thick soled Mary Janes. Her short curly gray hair was neatly styled. She looked friendly, bordering on old-fashioned grandmotherly when grandmothers looked the way they were supposed to. She was waiting for me to finish taking my picture. My finger froze as I clicked the button for the photo. She was going to accuse me of something, but what? She was going to reprimand me for something, but why?

The woman waited for me to complete my photos and put my phone back in my purse. I looked at her uncertainly. In a friendly voice and with a lovely warm smile she asked, "Are you interested in our concealed carry purses? We have a whole wall of them in the back of the booth. Why don't you let me show you around. We have several sizes and we are considered the best provider in the industry." That familiar feeling I had often experienced since arriving in Texas crept up my neck, like I was in an alien country. I thought, "There's an entire industry around something I never even knew was a 'thing'?" Without thinking about it, my natural curiosity took over. I was genuinely interested in the sociology and anthropology of these things. I said, "Yes! Thank you!" I was so ill-versed in the ways of Texas, let alone Texas women, I really had no idea what concealed carry meant.

"I'm new to Texas," I said. "I don't really know what concealed carry is about or any kind of carry."

"Well, honey," she replied. "Come on back inside the booth and let me show you what we have and why we are the best." The booth was beautifully laid out, much like a high end boutique, with artfully placed displays and good lighting. About fifty purses in the same cheerful, feminine fabrics hung on the wall. The lesson began.

"The reason our concealed carry bags are considered the best in the industry is not only because they are beautiful and beautifully made, but they look so natural. Most concealed carry purses are leather and designed to facilitate a three step motion. Step one is to reach inside the purse and unzip or unsnap the pouch with the gun. Step two is to grasp the gun and pull it out. Step three is to either then stand and shoot or go down on one knee and shoot. Watch me." She demonstrated smoothly and expertly.

"Now *our* bags bring you to safety in just two moves. Watch me again," she said. She placed one of the bags over her left shoulder. "One!" In one motion, she reached across her chest while plunging her hand into an interior pocket secured with Velcro. Then stepping forward one step with her right leg, she pulled out her hand from the bag, extended her right arm with her hand in the universal "bang bang" gun position at some perceived target in the distance and shouted, "Two!" Then, "Bang!"

"You see," she patiently explained after regaining her friendly grandmotherly stance with her hands in the pockets of her jumper, "our competitors are three step motion. You have to open the slot where the gun pocket is, which is either snapped or zipped. Ours is Velcro and designed so your hand fits in there without having to do anything, eliminating that first time consuming step that can cost you your life. What you just saw is our innovative and preferable two-step method." Hmmm. There it was again. The Two-Step. This was another version of moving from slow-slow to quick-quick.

I've had a great deal of professional marketing training and practical experience, and the case she made for her product, as well as her presentation itself, was impressive, and completely at odds with her appearance. Maybe that was the genius of her presentation. She could be anyone's grandmother or mother. She could be me, although I'd never wear that get up. She finished her presentation to the applause of the rest of the women in the booth and on the porch who had stopped fondling the colorful quilted bags, watching carefully. No one was joking or laughing. My salesperson grandma in the flowery dress was now surrounded by women asking questions about pricing, style, and delivery time. It left me wondering what I'd just witnessed and what it meant, to me, the State of Texas, and the state of the country. Had I missed a huge memo over the last few decades wrapped in my blue bubble?

What had started out as another eyeroll Texas joke sobered me up quickly. I left without a purchase but not before wondering if it wouldn't be a good idea to have one "just in case," both the purse and the gun to go into it. And I guess, really, that was the bottom line of her marketing campaign – her and the gun industry's – to leave me wondering if I needed such a thing, the fashionable conceal purse, and the gun. This is exactly what I'd been afraid of. I'd have to think about these crazy, terrifying things even at the market on a beautiful Saturday morning, and I didn't want to think about these things. But clearly a lot of people already were.

I was around gun talk all the time. I discovered even my alma mater in God's Left Elbow, Texas Tech, has this hand thing with that gun thing (Index finger and thumb extended making the hand look like a gun) with which 50,000 students salute each other and urge their teams on with a "Guns Up!" during football games. I suppose the "Hook 'Em Horns" The

University of Texas had used for eons was too much to take in this new era of big business football. It's all about what looks good on the big screens. I find it weird and off-putting, and frankly silly. Luckily, I'm so old the Guns Up! gesture didn't even exist when I was at Texas Tech.

So, this is how it starts, my reintroduction to Texas. My stomach clenched. I left the gun purse booth to meet up with my friend for some terrific barbeque and to pick up the specialty cactus I had bought earlier at another booth, but the rest of the experience that morning wasn't the same. The combat camouflage material here was not the typical green and brown of the hunter's jumpsuit or the military, rather, Liberty of London and Laura Ashley, designed to conceal weapons in pastels and flowers, making it easier to accept the rhythm of shooting as just another two-step.

I did send the photo of the yellow sign outside of the market booth to my blue state friends, knowing they would accelerate their plot to extract me from Texas. I was not going to discourage them. It couldn't be fast enough. But for now, I had to make do. It could only get better. It's all good, right?

Guns up!

I'm Sassy, Sweet, and Packing Heat

Unpublished Lyrics and Music by Chick Morgan @2014

I just came home to Texas, haven't lived here in a while
Didn't take long to learn what new bling could make me smile
I asked around and drove downtown, sure wasn't hard to see
There's a new kind of store with goodies galore
With some shiny accessories.

I'm sassy, sweet, and packing heat
Got my boots and I'm looking for fun
I just rolled into Texas
Now I'm a diva with a gun.

I'm learning how girls work it here in Texas
Which fashion's a must, which to ignore
'Bout boots and bling, which firearm to carry
Girls outside of Texas just ignore
I'm a fashionista legend now in Texas
Know how to dress with style when I need fun
I coordinate for every date in Texas
Pearl earrings, pearl necklace, and pearl handled guns. (Chorus)

The Arrival

14 – The Poorly Wrapped Gift

The very things that hold you down are going to lift you up.

~ Timothy Mouse
in the film *Dumbo*, 1949

As usual, the traffic heading south from Wimberley to San Antonio inched along, the late morning sun streaming uncomfortably in the driver seat window. The bottleneck getting to the familiar turnoff of the Interstate and onto the access road had not changed. In fact, it had gotten worse over the intervening seven years, so there I sat. The gravel trucks still spewed their rocks and a tricked out pickup truck as big as a ranch house gunned his big V-8 and blasted Miranda Lambert and Elle King's "Drunk (And I Don't Want to Go Home)" into the heat of the day.

The trip from Wimberley to the Army Residence Community still felt familiar, even though I had not made the journey in the seven years since Daddy died. Sitting there waiting for the afternoon traffic to start moving again brought memories of the last time I was at the ARC. Daddy's memorial service. The service had been in the ARC Chapel and internment was in Fort Sam Houston National Cemetery where he was buried with Mom. His coffin was already draped with the American flag by the time the family arrived at the assigned kiosk in the cemetery. Only the number on the kiosk identified the location from the others in the massive cemetery. A small contingent of Masonic brothers from the Army Lodge Daddy had been a member of for decades, ultimately rising to Grand Master, was there, ready to read the Masonic portion of the service.

With me that day at Daddy's memorial service was Totally
Inappropriate Bad Boy Boyfriend who'd flown in from Phoenix
the night before. He'd kept a bag packed by his door ready to
go on an instant's notice as soon as he heard from me. That was
so like him. We'd reconnected several years prior, but his presence only added to the strain and sorrow of the day. I was
planning to end the relationship (again) the next day.

I was angry at the minister-for-hire from hospice who arrived
in a short-sleeved shirt. Every other man there was in a full suit
and tie or dress uniform and polished shoes, July in Texas or
not. For Christ's sake it was a military funeral. I felt embarrassed my father did not get the respect he'd earned at this
moment. I knew for certain he was watching, appalled and
furious, and was probably giving someone Hell up in Heaven
right now.

After the homilies and rituals there was a fifteen-gun salute
followed by a bugler who played Taps. I am a military kid to my
core and Taps affects me to my core. Its plaintive notes remind
me of the many nights I listened to them chiming from the
Quadrangle during those years living across the street from the
historic fort. Paradoxically, the lingering note at the end of each
phrase, and the "God is nigh" conclusion drifting slowly towards Heaven, also reminds me of summer GA camp in the
Blue Ridge mountains where each of us ten year old campers
assembled on the porch of our cabin in our pajamas and sang
each phrase cabin by cabin.

> *Day is done, gone the sun*
> *From the lakes from the hills from the*
> *sky All is well, safely rest*
> *God is nigh*

My brothers had decided earlier in the day they wanted me to receive Daddy's flag at the interment, which I tearfully did. At the conclusion of the service as I left the kiosk, I stopped at the casket. Laying both hands on the highly polished surface I said my final, personal goodbye to Daddy. I wanted him to know I would not have traded one minute of the last two years in Texas for all the world. But he already knew.

I was on my way to another memorial service at the ARC that hot late morning stuck in traffic. My car still knew the route and all the visual markers as if it were yesterday. I noted how many new buildings had gone up along the side roads. A disorienting battle of the familiar and the new was working its way from my brain down to my heart, much like the internal struggle of ambivalence I'd waged for all the years since my return to Texas. I rounded the last corner and saw the tower of the ARC looming ahead, triggering a sweet sadness and melancholy comfort.

The bluebonnets were in bloom. Like so many other trips returning to Wimberley after being with Daddy at the ARC, I knew the thick blankets of blue along the roads and up the hillsides on my trip home would provide a welcome balm for my sadness. I was overcome with emotion making the turn onto O'Connor Road. So many memories, most of them happy memories of being with parents well cared for in a well-run place they loved and had many friends. We should all be so fortunate.

The Rev. Dr. Colonel Gene Allen had been chaplain of the Protestant Chapel at the ARC almost the entire time I used to visit my parents. He was dynamic, charismatic, and charming, with a skewering sense of humor and brilliant mind. The fading evidence of significant facial injuries and scars from his wounds

resulting from hostile fire conducting a Christmas Eve service
in Vietnam resulted in a speech impairment that required me
and others to listen intently to his words, which we all did, for
they were never to be missed.

Gene and his stunningly beautiful wife Brenda, a successful real
estate agent in San Antonio, had become good friends to
Mother and Daddy. Daddy adored both Gene and Brenda, and
being in their presence made my mother come alive in a way I
seldom witnessed. Over the years, Gene and Brenda and I
developed our own special relationship, and Gene and I would
often meet for an early coffee in the lobby of the ARC on the
days I was visiting. He had a huge appetite for the world. He
loved to talk about my international consulting career, the work
I was doing in Russia and Central Europe, and my research and
books on cross-cultural business ethics. He loved New York
and Broadway and always wanted to hear about my latest
shows. He was a satisfying, wide-ranging conversation partner
in current events, politics, history, ethics, and spirituality who
always left me with a couple of excellent jokes – some I could
even repeat. The Irish philosopher and poet John O'Donohue
once described a friend of his as having "a well-furnished
mind." I felt that way about Gene. He reminded me with
affirmations and reassurances how much my parents were loved
by so many people in their community, including him and
Brenda. I came away from time with him feeling like I was a
better person, had a more open heart, and life – and God –
were good.

Even though I had not seen him in several years and had
intuited from Brenda's Facebook postings that he was quite ill,
the news of his death surprised me. I was happy she had
personally invited me to his memorial service. I went alone. I
felt anxiety, uncertainty, and a strong apprehension of opening

old wounds from the past in anticipation of being back at the ARC for another celebration of life for someone so intercomnected with my life and my parents' life. Would the memories of that difficult Day of Double Barreled Heartbreak rush in again and burst open in a similar mess as my Red Lobster and Drury Inn mess? The longer I sat in traffic on that hot morning, more memories rushed in of those early difficult days and weeks, all the more overwhelming since the day I vowed to be with my father and then get out of Texas again.
But here I was. Still in Texas.

The traffic eventually eased enough for me to arrive at the ARC Chapel and make my way into the familiar sanctuary full of joyful ghosts and music I had sung over the years. Sitting in the Chapel, listening to each of the loving, heartwarming speakers unspooling stories of Gene's remarkable life, I began to think about how my own life would be different if I had not decided to live in Wimberley to be with Daddy, throwing myself into self-reinvention while I still had some years with him. Weddings and funerals will do that to you, make you look at your own life more carefully and honestly. At my age I have been to a lot of both.

I had calculated it would take two years for Daddy to die, and it was pretty close to that. Of course, I was going to be in Saudi Arabia for two months every other two months, and that didn't work out. What part did that turn of fate at the last minute play in where I ended up? In my original plan, Daddy's death was supposed to be the trigger to call the POD moving company again, put my house on the market, crank up my consulting network and client base and let them know I was back in the game more aggressively than ever, have some lunches and some "I'm leaving" glasses of wine, get the car serviced, gassed up, and head out again – somewhere. That was the plan. Boris

Pasternak said, "When a great moment knocks on the door of your life, it is often no louder than the beating of your heart, and it is very easy to miss it."

I suspect I had many knocks on the door of my life over those first two years back in Texas, and it would have been very easy to miss them. Why hadn't I? Once I had decided to say YES I grabbed opportunities flying by me as fast as a quarter horse racing at Ruidoso Downs.

Many of my morning readings during those early days on the road were from Buddhist teachings, which include the four principles:

- Show up
- Speak the truth
- Do what you do with enthusiasm
- Don't get attached to the outcome

Mine became a modified version of those principles to get me through one day at a time:

- Get up (some days the hardest part)
- Get dressed (some days I couldn't remember why)
- Show up (somewhere, just because it's important)
- Speak up (about something)

Even today friends and former colleagues say, "How can you stand living in Texas after all the places you've lived?" I have to correct them that I came back to Texas but I ended up in Wimberley. Gradually I learned that Wimberley really is all about the arts, the arts are all intertwined, and once I met one or two people, I seemed to automatically know ten others. People wanted me involved in their organizations and then pretty soon be on the board of one thing or another, all of which meant meeting more people, interesting people interested in things I'm interested in.

At the time, my sister-in-law was involved in the Wimberley Art League. She was also a volunteer at The Visitor Center run by a very savvy and competent woman who also ran the Chamber of Commerce. Cathy was a driving force behind everything pro-active and interesting (at least to me) in Wimberley. Just being in her orbit meant I probably knew everything that was exciting and potentially interesting (at least to me) going on in town. When Cathy suggested you get involved, you did. We all loved to help her out, get involved, and within six months I was in a circle of provocative new neighbors and artists of many kinds — musicians, painters, sculptors, writers, chefs, wood workers, and songwriters.

Not long after I arrived I was shopping in the local grocery store with my sister-in-law when she said, "Come over here with me to the bread aisle. I just spotted someone I need to talk to about a stretching class she's thinking of giving in her studio." Her name was Lee and she ran a musical theater and voice training organization in town for young children through high school age. She projected an enormous energy and a personality that was six feet tall on her 4' 10" frame.

Lee was a force. I went home that day and looked up her website. She'd just begun a new enterprise in her musical performance company in Wimberley, The Black Diamond Cabaret. She was looking to stage cabaret performers in special evening events. Cabaret in Wimberley? Hold on! I curbed my excitement and enthusiasm for many months hoping not to get my hopes and high NYC expectations ahead of whatever reality was opening up. I ended up presenting two evenings of a two-act full-on New York cabaret style show later that year. It wasn't on Broadway or Off-Broadway or 46th Street, but it was a professional show in a beautiful historic building with a beautiful old stage, something I thought I'd never do again.

When I think about the awful early days of my road trip culminating in my life here, in a place I always thought I never wanted to be, I understand these years have been my roadmap for becoming who I always was. The songwriter John Gorka, at the beginning of one of his four day songwriting retreats when asked about why he still teaches said, "I'm always learning what I used to know."

I always knew I was "the little girl with musical talent;" "so creative;" "a good writer;" "smart." For most of my life those labels felt like they should have an asterisk. The creativity seeped through and bled around the edges in ways that kept them present to people in my life but never seemed to me to be about my real life.

A curious thing started happening a decade earlier when I began intentionally defining myself as an artist in the midst of my corporate work. A few years after I began singing on stage in New York, I added what I thought was a throw-away line to the bottom of my one page bio:

"When Morgan is not attending to her organizational day job, she's a New York cabaret singer and performer." As soon as I started adding that line, someone, some executive in every group I worked with, would come up and ask me about my singing, and then add:

> *I used to play the flute in the high school band, and I loved it.*
> *I used to sing in my church choir and I miss it.*

I shared with each of them the pivotal moment in my life, in my 50s, when I claimed a small portion of my creative and artistic life. I came home one day and announced to my husband, "I'm tired of defining myself as someone who used to sing." I had come across a line attributed to Oliver Wendell Holmes, Jr.: "Most people go to their grave with their music still inside them." I vowed at that moment not to be one of them. It was still a sideline but it was out there as at least part of who I am. I still defined myself as a corporate design, strategy, and leadership consultant for Fortune 500 companies, but I also defined myself as a singer. Some clients were obviously confused. One elegant English executive stood before his leadership team in London in his very British dark-blue wide-pin-striped suit and light-blue wider-pin-striped shirt and introduced me: "Morgan is not only a corporate strategy consultant but a Pole Dancer, too!"

Today I define myself as a creative artist, an arts entrepreneur, producer, singer-songwriter, cabaret performer, podcaster, radio host, and writer. I need a big business card these days.

As I sat in the ARC Chapel celebrating Gene Allen's life, I traced the journey that brought me to the place of creating a life defined as an artist. To be honest, I still have issues and uncomfortable differences with a lot of the political and cultural elements so prominent in the state and in the national news, but I am also more aware every day of the gifts in my life because I came here.

If I hadn't come to Texas I would not be a singer-songwriter. In my New York cabaret days I had a friend who kept insisting, "Why don't *you* write songs? You should do it!" She pestered me about it for years and even gifted me books about songwriting, all of which I promptly ignored, stashing the books in the back of a bookshelf. In Wimberley I met other musicians and song-writers who helped me. In Wimberley there are many music venues to sing these songs, and I did.

If I hadn't come to Texas I would never have created The Cash-mere Cowgirls, a "girl band" with semi-adequate music skills, great song choices (including mine), and personality to burn, a huge hit in town, and known for "Music with Attitude." A few years later it would be creating a classy duo, Women With Standards, singing the American Songbook and Contemporary Standards Songbook as we developed a passionate following in the region.

If I hadn't come to Texas I might have never had my own radio program on a local radio station, a combination of music and interviews which I loved doing and was really good at, as I suspected I might be. The radio program led to cohosting a well-regarded podcast a few years later with an internationally renowned and awarded wildlife photographer.

If I hadn't come to Texas I might not have been on some excellent arts boards and been tapped to produce the Wimberley Alive! Music and Arts Festival. I learned I loved producing events and being the Grand Puppeteer. Every shred of my thirty-five years of corporate leadership and strategy experience was put to use.

If I hadn't come to Texas I might never have experienced how a town can come together and hold each other up by sheer force of intent, determination and love, digging out friends and strangers' homes and lives submerged in mud, day after day, week after week. Ruined homes and all of us aghast at the total

devastation of long sections of one of our proud and beautiful
rivers stripped bare of many of the centuries old cypress trees
because a forty foot wall of water going one hundred miles an
hour raced through, sweeping trees, homes, taking lives with it,
the subsequent quiet even louder than the storm. Big, destruct-
tive, horrific events happen anywhere, unfortunately. And do.
In a small town it happens to everyone, to all of us, all at once. I
was constantly asked by friends outside of Wimberley, "Were
you affected by the flood?" My answer, as honest as I could
make it, was, "My house is fine. But we are *all* affected by it."
Nothing in my life has ever been truer – or the same.

If I hadn't come to Texas I would not have discovered my own
family in time. My older brother Mike has been my quiet hero
my whole life. His irrepressible nature and his irredeemably
quick, smart, bad (and legendary) sense of humor, his unques-
tionable sense of integrity and fairness, had already forged a
path with my equally remarkable sister-in-law in this town.
Arriving in Wimberley at the time I did with a half empty POD
but a trailer load of emotional wreckage in my wake, I was given
an unexpected gift of getting to know both of them. It was odd
and wonderful to hear the words, "This is my sister, Chick." I
hadn't been called Chick by anyone other than my family in
over forty years and only when I was visiting Texas. Mike and
I went to cut a live Christmas tree my first year here, the first
live tree I'd had in over twenty years since His Nibs couldn't be
bothered with Christmas trees, or Christmas in general. We
went to a family owned lot in the next town over. It was
freezing cold that day with high winds, but we took our time.
He strapped my tree on the top of my car. At home he cut the
angle on the base of the trunk the way Daddy taught us and put
it in a bucket of water on my back porch until I was ready to
bring it indoors to decorate.

I have spent more time than I ever had with my younger
brother, Ken, even though he lives in Midland, a good five or
six hours away. This is Texas, remember. He and I are very
different, but I would walk on hot coals for him and I think he
would for me. Even though Ken is six years younger than me,
he has always been another big brother to me. Those years
together, dealing with Mom's death, Daddy's dementia and
death, gave the three of us the knowledge that when the chips
were down, we were there for Mother and Daddy, and we were
there for each other.

If I hadn't come to Texas I would not know that the worst days of
my life can ease and morph into something pretty wonderful
over time if I trust my heart and take some chances and be
open to The Yes, whether out of temporary helplessness or
direct intention, which I had a little of some and a lot of both.
One day it occurred to me that the oak is also the symbol of
Celtic spirituality and here in the Hill Country I am surrounded
by the beautiful live oaks. Ireland is truly my second and spiritual home, not just for the well-lauded emerald beauty, but
because it's the deep spiritual center of my own creativity. Now,
here I sit, squarely in the midst of them – the oaks, I mean.

If I hadn't come to Texas I might not have discovered what is
essential for me in creating a community of artists, intellects,
and friends who deeply inspire me, encourage me, challenge me,
open doors, and help me understand who I am at my core –
and still love me. That community is the Blue Rock Artist
Ranch and Recording Studio here in Wimberley, Texas, and the
Blue Rock Foundation, of which I am now a board member. I
walk through the doors of the beautiful home of Dodee and
Billy Crockett who dreamed it and manifested it into a stunning
home and studio. I breathe easier, my anticipation heightens,
and a sense of joy spontaneously wells up. I've heard dozens of

musical artists during years of concert series. I've learned the craft of songwriting participating in the legendary songwriter retreat weekends with some of the most respected names in the business. I've had sustained conversations of the spirit over the years I've been a part of it. Of all the things I know would not have happened if I had not come to Texas, that one I know for sure. I can't imagine my life today without it and the friends who inspire and support me.

All of these things have been extraordinary gifts in my life, which I have received with the heartbreak, upheaval, heaviness, and hard work of reinvention; gifts which I may never have been the recipient of without the words:

If I only have fifteen more years to live, I don't want to live them in this relationship.

Hard, hard words to hear and still hard to remember, words whose effect has blunted somewhat, but will never be entirely forgotten. Gifts, nevertheless, no matter how poorly wrapped they came.

These days I am asked why I've stayed in Texas. It's complicated, like most relationships. Some days the answer is easy and honest, days when my music and writing consume me, and there are friends at the end of the day for a glass of wine. There is the love of a long-legged handsome Texan who happens to be one of those long-ago Texas relationships I rediscovered after working together for months on an arts committee. We share a love of the Hill Country, our gentle dogs, a beautiful home with flaming Hill Country sunsets easing us out of day. We also share a childhood upbringing in the military and all that that means. And *that* story deserves its own lengthier telling which is in progress as I write. But some days the question of why I've stayed, and its answer, feels harder, when I feel so far from Paris, when the oceans' rhythms lapping the shore on either coast are too distant for me to hear.

As I age I am more aware of the importance of friends and grateful to still have the time to connect, enjoy, and grow from these relationships. Maybe that's what His Nibs was trying to express in his ham-fisted way, his awareness of aging and time going by and needing to spend whatever time he thought he might have left with people – or a person – who nourished him in ways I could not.

As I age I'm aware of my vulnerability in other ways. I'm old enough to know my heart can break and heal again, no matter how much time it requires. I'm aware of trying to live with honesty, and acknowledge its companion, vulnerability, as much as I can. I have the good fortune of good genes and health and don't take that for granted for a second.

As I age I understand I am vulnerable to a whole new assort-ment of physical challenges and prospects – arbitrary falls, memory loss, new health issues or syndromes of diseases that can creep up on me with that aging. The accompanying vulnerability always comes with the questions: Who will be there for me in those times? My friends? Certainly, and I for them. But the reality is we are all getting older. 2 a.m. runs to the Emergency Room thirty miles away become less a given in my cadre of friends and acquaintances, especially with no family of blood close by. The realities of those two things closing in, aging and vulnerability, were the first assaults that slammed me when I got that phone call on the morning my mother died. Some of that feeling – that threat – is always present.

These questions greet me in the morning, usually when I'm sleepless at 4 a.m. I find myself wondering, as I did when I was a child and living in different towns and countries as an Army Kid, where is my home, really? Am I finally at home here in the Hill Country of Texas? Once again, a line from a hymn from my Southern Baptist days crossed my mind:

"This world is not my home, I'm just a' passin' through."

I used to think that about Texas when I came back here, that I was just passing through. If I'm still passing through why am I still here? If I'm just passing through what do I know about where I might be heading?

This World Is Not My Home

Anonymous 1919

This world is not my home, I'm just a-passing through
My treasures are laid up somewhere beyond the blue
The angles beckon me from Heaven's open door
And I can't feel at home in this world anymore

Chorus:

Oh, Lord, you know I have no friend like You
If Heaven's not my home, then Lord what will I do?
The angels beckon me from heaven's open door
And I can't feel at home in this world anymore

15 – Home Room. Home Base. Home.

And what you thought you came for is only a shell,
a husk of meaning.

~ T. S. Eliot, "Little Gidding"

If not the whispered longing and innate wisdom of our own hearts,
what and who will ever call us home to ourselves anymore?

~ John Cabot-Zinn

As I turned the key into my new home in Wimberley, Texas I wondered:

Is it more important to have a home, a home base, feel at home somewhere, or be at home with myself?

"Where are you from?" a new friend in Wimberley asked. As usual, I was stumped. For most anyone else other than an Army brat, it's a simple question. For me, and most military kids, the circumstances of your birth are arbitrary. Where was your dad stationed at the moment your mother dilated to ten centimeters? For me, it was Washington, D.C., not even a state. That made me even more suspect.

My mother came from a small town in southwest Virginia where her people were tobacco farmers for hundreds of years. My dad from Richmond. They both left in their teens with their families of birth. Does that make me a girl of the deep south? Yes and no. Is it "home?" Not really.

Where are you from?

Does that make me the dreaded "Yankee?" Yes and no. Does it make me a Texan? Depends on who's asking.

As Tennyson put it, so well, in fact, I used it as the title of one of my New York cabaret shows: I am "roaming with a hungry heart."

Up to the moment before I got the phone call from my husband on the Day of Double Barreled Heartbreak, I had co-owned a home with a husband. What could home mean when I transitioned from my teenage bedroom to my college dorm being married three times over all my years, most recently in a sixteen-yearlong committed, loving relationship. His Nibs and I created several homes together over those years. Now I was single and moving towards, well, what exactly? Where exactly?

As a child I remember learning about the hermit crab. It lives in the shells of other creatures at the beach, moving to bigger shells as it grows. It carries whatever it can on its back, finds a new abandoned shell, and moves in. I know there are birds that use other birds' nests rather than building their own. My family, and every other family I knew growing up, lived in "quarters," housing provided on post by the Army rather than individually owned private homes. It was not only the norm, but it was also all I knew. Within a narrow range, depending on rank and availability, houses were identical. One family moved on to the next assignment, and after a quick paint job and thorough cleaning a new one moved in. We rarely hung pictures. Nail holes had to be repaired before moving again. We never painted

262

the walls. It wasn't allowed. I don't recall anyone having a garden. Somehow, tiny tendrils of individuality and personality sprouted anyway; a new bedspread and matching pillows; a new sofa and area rug; framed family photos on any surface that would support them.

As I turned the key into my new home in Wimberley, Texas, I wondered:

Is it more important to have a home, have a home base, feel at home somewhere, or be at home with my myself?

I stood at my new front door and paused. I was almost sixty-four without a home of my own. How was I lesser or freer or "more" or different from the woman who was contentedly coupled in a home that felt sweet and close and loving and dear and mine? It was a big part of what I had wanted to find out when I set out on the road trip journey.

What does home mean to me at sixty-four?

Thinking about home triggered memories of the importance of the home room we kids were assigned once we were high enough in the academic stratosphere to have classes in more than one room. A few days before school began for the year we would receive postcards from school telling us whose home room we were assigned. The teacher in the home room was almost as important as who else was included in it. My friends and I immediately dashed for the one black telephone in the hallway of our quarters to compare notes and hope against hope we were all together. It seldom worked out completely to our satisfaction, but usually enough of us were in the same home room to feel excited about the prospects of the opening bell and a sense of relief we would have the security of a couple of good friends. Home room was where we started each day. I could share notes with my friends, whisper about our class-mates, who had just had a fight with whom? Who broke up over the weekend? Who started going out together? Home room was the place we gathered in an emergency or even a simple change in our on-going routine. It was our anchor in our school world, populated by our friends and hopefully a favorite teacher to witness our lives.

I was also thinking about home base, any home base, or, more correctly, home plate. It's the place we begin to try to make our mark, get a hit, steal a base, and score a point in life. I can't score a point unless I round the bases and end the drive again at home base. I am aware at my age of a circularity to my life now. Comings and goings. Fits and starts. Back to familiar places that heal my soul and friends who help me make sense of life, what-ever sense is to be found. Round the bases.

Dorothy knew. Home was Kansas until she woke up looking into the worried loving eyes of family and friends. Then she knew "there's no place like home." If only I could click my red heels like Dorothy and know where home is. Can I just find someone who "has to take me in when I need a place to go," as Robert Frost asked? I certainly found people who took me in for six months when I had no place to go. Each of those homes, because of the love and connections, felt like mine for a short while.

I want a home base from which I can move forward. I want a landing field to return to when I spread my wings and create a new life in a strange town and an even stranger state. How can I fly without a landing field to return to? Can I really have a journey if there is no home to return to? Is home something that is external within whose walls I find quiet, rest and sleep? Is it my creative spirit, inclination towards hospitality, the Texas Grit I carry with me that I bring forth and share and which becomes a multiplier of the best of who I am, we are, what we stand for, how we love and what we have to give each other? And what do I have to give that makes me feel I am home? I was beginning to know.

I think the most important journeys are those where I venture out into the unknown, out of my comfort zones and my habits, with faith in myself to make the journey, where I grow and become different from who I was before I started, and have someone to share it with when I walk back through my door, closing it securely behind me.

I used to think genuine mythic journeys belonged only to the gods and goddesses of the mythologies – Greek, Roman, Irish, Indigenous. But they also belong to me, I see now.

My journey from that day beginning so many years ago had all the ingredients:

- A life altering incident to launch the journey (The Day of Double Barreled Heartbreak)
- Personal tests along the way (Would I live? How to live? Where to live?)
- Obstacles to overcome (Fears of abandonment, failure, ruin)
- Transformation and growth (Oh, my yes.)

All that was missing was the return. But return to what? By now I knew it was Texas, at least for a while. Why had I been so reluctant?

I was reluctant because I hated the idea of Texas, or so I thought. I didn't want to leave my beautiful home in Connecticut and beautiful life in Connecticut and New York and Santa Barbara. I didn't want my carefully curated public and self-perception of a sophisticated, intelligent, accomplished East Coast professional and cabaret artist to be diminished because I was returning to the perceived cultural wasteland I'd escaped over forty years ago. I didn't want all of that to be publicly wrapped up in the story of repeated relationship failures. I had experienced all of those fears in small chunks when I'd returned for visits over the years. I played it to the hilt. I felt like the Seinfeld character J. Peterman, the self-important swash-buckling world traveler with a story for everything from his leather fedora to his world famous friends. I found myself starting a sentence one time, "When I was in Czechoslovakia waiting for the solider, his rifle slung over his shoulder, and his German shepherd to pass our small group looking like we were on a picnic but actually having a meeting of another sorts…" Or, "I wanted to get to the U.S.S.R. in time before my meeting to see Yeltsin standing on the tank, but I missed it by a day." Or, "I was excited that beautiful clear fall day, the day I was walking up Sixth Avenue in New York City to Simon and Schuster to drop off my manuscript." I enjoyed my life. I loved my beautiful city clothes. I couldn't imagine not living life *that* large. I was wrong.

My return to Texas had very little to do with Texas. Surprise.

It had everything to do with being sixty-four years old, down on my luck in my professional life, down to rock bottom in my personal life, and with ragged breath, pounding heart, and tears waiting impatiently for release when the quiet moments came, flailing emotionally with the loss of my mother. In an instant I spun from knowing who I was, who I was loved by, where I lived and was going to live. In a single sixty second phone call I felt loss, I felt fear, I felt vulnerable in every way imaginable. I felt homeless.

I have always been an artist. It took me sixty-four years to recognize it. I am home – I am at home – as an artist. I thank my happenstance arrival in Texas, and this little town, for letting me see that. Reluctantly, yes, but seeing.

After the Mother-of-All-Downsizings several years previously with the sale of The Manor Born, what did I end up keeping in this second downsizing of my heart?

I kept my self-respect. I never demonized the man who dropped The Great Shitstorm on me. I let myself hurt and be angry, but it was about me, just like it had to be about my mother those weeks after her death and before her memorial service. I never demanded my friends "take sides." I never wished a slow painful death on him, neither did I overtly wish him happiness. I never wailed to have him come back, nor did I send a sympathy card when the Montecito house got destroyed in the Santa Barbara mudslides years later. I have boundaries. I have limits.

There was only one moment I came close to hating him: at my daughter-of-affection's wedding the following year. My daughter, her husband to be, and her mother, and her husband-to-be's entire family were extraordinarily gracious to me, making sure to include me in conversations and introducing me to family members I had not met.

The wedding was beautiful, held on a perfect northern California afternoon on a flower farm overlooking the Pacific Ocean. When I think of that day I still feel the slightly cool air on my skin. I see the riot of colors of the flowers on the hillsides and the deep blue of the distant ocean. I see the colorful dresses of the wedding party and guests and the white chairs set up in neat rows in front of a flower covered white arbor.

I had been invited to be in the wedding party, a huge honor, escorted by my daughter's soon-to-be brother-in-law. My heart sang. After the ceremony and after all the guests had walked to the top of the rise near where the ceremony occurred, the rounds of family photographs began. The bride and groom. The bride and groom and the groom's family. And then, "All of the Melvilles up here, please!" I stood off to the side, alone, as "all the Melvilles," my daughter and her husband, her mother, her father, her uncle, aunt, and niece, and her other uncle gathered in closely for the photos. I ached. For one desolate minute I fumbled self-consciously with my hands, finally grabbing my elbows, holding them close to my chest. As the photographer snapped away, positioning family members in different formations and clusters, a stab of recognition so deep and irreparable took my breath away for several seconds. He took my family. God damn him.

Later in the family photo round robin, my daughter's new father-in-law, a former Naval Commander, and her new mother-in-law, insisted I join them in a family photo with her husband's siblings and wives.

"Morgan!" He said authoritatively. "Come here and stand between me and Irene," his wife. I demurred.

"That's okay, John. I'll stand here at the end."

"No you will not," he said, evenly, more authoritatively, every
bit the former Naval Commander. So, of course, I did come
stand next to him and between him and his wife. None of them
will ever know how much that single gesture meant to me.
Kindness completely undoes me and in spite of what I'd been
through I realize there is much kindness in my world. I remain
closely connected to my daughter and son-in-law and her uncle
and aunt and niece on her Dad's side. I kept the best of all of
them. The years since continue to prove that to be true.

I've come to believe that home is sometimes a verb, not a noun.
A few years ago a small, honey-colored miniature, long-haired
dachshund came into our home, my Sweetie's and mine, by way
of some vet friends in the neighborhood. He is adorable. Total
perfection, actually, if you ask me, his mom, and I can't imagine
this part of my life without him. In the vernacular of the animal
world he is a "re-home," his original family several states away
no longer able to care for him. I would like to think that this
time in my life and my return to Texas has been another kind of
"re-homing." We don't use the word "home" as a verb unless it
is coupled with "re," and in the coming back into another home
we may find ourselves.

So you see, I did come back to claim my whole life – and create
a new one. It looks different than I'd been trained to believe it
would look growing up. It is not husband centric or couple
centric, although those things add up for many people to make
a life. It is passion centric, artist centric, creative centric. As long
as I am still moved by music, writing, songwriting, and two-
stepping, and curious about your heart and stories, I know I am
home. I experience my longing for these things and more as a
welcome friend, not a frustrating intruder.

My good friend Billy Crockett, songwriter and producer, co-creator of the magical Blue Rock Artist Ranch and Studio in Wimberley, said one time after a songwriter retreat:

> *I feel so strongly that 'it' is still out there for me – whatever it is that I am in this for and doing all this for – whatever 'it' is – I am still living into it.* (And so am I.)

John O'Donohue, Irish philosopher and poet, said, "Longing is our heart's prompting and reminder that we already know where we belong and who and what brings us alive."

What brings me alive is a community that has allowed me to flourish as I'm aging. My longing to survive, to live, to create a new path brought me to Texas, reluctantly. Texas brought me home to myself, the artist, the songwriter, the writer, the two-stepper. And for now at least, it is here. In Wimberley. As Rumi advised, I have indeed "set myself on fire and surrounded myself with people who fan the flames."

So, it was never about Texas, really. Recently on a beautiful Hill Country evening, the full moon shining between the branches of a large live oak tree on the terrace of a familiar restaurant listening to one of my favorite music groups, drinking a chilled glass of more than average white wine, sitting among a couple of tables of people I have come to love and enjoy, a light breeze blowing, I thought, "What if I stayed here forever?" It's a thought, anyway. That night, a pleasant one. "Here" is not necessarily Texas, although it might be. It is, I know now, the peace I've found as an artist. It is looking at my life as a continuing journey in resilience, off-roading every day in some way to create joy – and just create. At long last I've finally found the line of dance.

Quick-quick.
Slow-slow.
Away I go.

Already Perfect

Lyrics and Music by Billy Crockett
© 2016 Spare Room Music

Keep thinking I'll get this right
I'm not going to get it
Got an infinite appetite
In spite of my limits
I wish I may I wish I might
That's the story of my life
But here and now tonight
It's already perfect.

Didn't want to be feeling small
Light as a feather
I wanted to knock that ball
Clean to forever
I can't see confetti fall
Down through the lights
But here and now tonight
It's already perfect

If I hadn't missed that train
If I had stayed in school
If I could stop the rain
If only I had prayed harder

Drop a coin in the wishing well
And you stare at the bottom
Nothing happens as far as you can tell
But wishes you got 'em
Snap out of this foolish spell

Go back to your life
'Cause here and now tonight
Yes it is.

Keep thinking about this life span
Like sparks in the firelight
Keep thinking 'bout grains of sand
Look up at the stars
I want you to hold my hand
Let's try to breath it in
'Cause here and now tonight
It's already perfect
It's already perfect

Gratitudes and Acknowledgements

One of the many gifts of aging is gaining an understanding of how many people, hearts, and words surround us throughout a long life, and if you are fortunate, as I am, deepen and enrich it. If you are a writer, as I am, those gifts come as encouragement, support, critique, and ears to listen, glasses of wine, retreat escapes to write in, shoulders to cry on, and very often, just the right word to keep going.

Some of those hearts and words and brains supply expertise in the craft of writing itself, including The Writers League of Texas. I met fellow writers in workshops, conferences, and classes over eight years, along with the talented and remarkably accessible staff led by the accomplished Becka Oliver. I owe a special thanks to author and class instructor Donna Johnson who was an early believer and encourager of my work.

I am grateful to Janna Marlies Marron and Karen Beattie of More to the Story who helped me set ambitious, rigorous deadlines, as well as provided detailed editing on structure and narrative arc. Their guidance and input made this a better book.

I am grateful to The Old Schoolers Writing Group, Gary Keith (and the ebullient Leslie Dusing), and Jeff and Rebecca Connally, for your helpful, honest critique, sometimes difficult conversations, community and friendship.

I am grateful to The Dancing Divas (Inese, Dede, Kay, Judith, Renee, and K.C.), our remarkable group of women who has witnessed each other's lives for twenty years and supported all my far-flung creative endeavors. You were there from the beginning, as usual.

I am grateful for the wonderful writers and creative friends in my hometown of Wimberley, Texas, including Wimberley Area Writers and the Wine and Words Group. There were early readers who asked the hard questions and highlighted the gaps in the narrative arc of these chapters: Patrick Cox, Ashley Brown, Deirdre Taylor, Denise Renter, Mary Lancaster, Judy Schell, Nathan Brown, Debbie Howard, Gayle Brown, Becky McCullough, and Monica Michell, Cynthia Beath, and Cathy Moreman. Thank you Dodee and Billy Crockett for upholding the gold standard of quality and excellence in the arts, and your unconditional support of me.

Thank you Meg Hartzler and Pam Dennis via Colorado, and Karen Workman and Susan Small via West Virginia. You are a brilliant cadre of women I am honored and grateful to know.

I am grateful to Joyce Maynard and our Lake Atitlan, Guatemala Write By the Lake group of thirteen women across the age span. Joyce, you made me a more skillful and empathic writer in one week as I listened to the stories from each of these amazing, talented women who remain a big part of my creative adventure. Thank you Fauntel, Danielle, Heather, Hannah, Jessica, Sara, Paula, Connie, Nancy, Linda, Elizabeth, and Kari Ella.

Thank you, thank you to my sweetie and two-stepping partner, Bob Smith, who created every writer's dream studio creative space for me, holding peace and quiet, with expansive views of birds, trees, sky, and even cows, a true Texas Hill Country little piece of heaven – all the inspiration I could want to keep writing. It's a2 perfect gift. Thank you.

I am very grateful to Mezcalita Press and their excellent editorial and creative team, especially Nathan Brown, Senior Executive Editor, for turning all those pages into a beautiful book. It's been a joyous experience.

Endnotes

Chapter 1

1. His Nibs: An important or self-important person, usually used in a phrase as if a title or honorific.

2. "My Mother's Dreams" words and music by Chick Morgan. YouTube: Wimberley Women with Standards

Chapter 2

3. Cabaret is an all-encompassing performance genre and can include singing styles from Broadway to jazz to folk music and everything in between. Accompanied by live piano, cabaret performers fully embrace the role of storyteller, embodying the varied themes and emotions of each song and story. There's no decorated set, high-lifted stage, or elaborate costumes; but this simplified approach to performance art removes the barrier between the audience and the performers. You aren't required to suspend any disbelief. Anyone can connect to the stories, songs, and performers on a personal level, listening, laughing, or even shedding a tear as the music moves them.

Chapter 3

4. Conscientious Objector (CO): One who is opposed to serving in the armed forces and/or bearing arms on the grounds of moral or religious principle.

Chapter 4

5. "Should I Stay or Should I Go?" The Clash. Lyrics by Joe Strummer. Album *Combat Rock,* 1982.

Chapter 5

6. "We've a Story to Tell to the Nations," written by Henry
    Ernest Nichol, first US printing 1908. It is the Girls
    Auxiliary Anthem.

Chapter 6

7. "Grey Divorce: Complete Guide to the Silver Splitters."
    Dalena & Bosch Attorneys at Law. August 26, 2021.

8. "The New Old Age: Who Will Care for the 'Kinless
    Seniors?'" by Paula Span, *The New York Times,* December
    2, 2022.

9. Wallowing: v. Present participle of wallow. 1) chiefly of
    large mammals – roll about or lie in mud or water,
    especially to keep cool avoiding biting insects, or spread
    scent 2) of a boat or aircraft – roll from side to side 3) to
    live self-indulgently; luxuriate; revel.

Chapter 7

10. In graduate school many years later I read literature in the
    new sciences that played with some elements of quantum
    physics. Out of all the books and journal articles, one
    thread remains with me: the impact of the observer on the
    observed. Every situation, communication, or interaction
    is impacted because of the *very act of observation.* A meme of
    quantum physics has come from Schrodinger's Cat. Is the
    cat in the box alive or dead? It's either one until you look
    into the box.

Chapter 9

11. Champagne Swords are now available on Amazon.com
    and make great party gifts.

Chapter 13

12. "Don't Forget the Guns." Words and music by Cheryl Wheeler @ 2014 Get Guns Direct.

13. Concealed carry is the practice of carrying a weapon (typically a handgun) on one's physical person while taking steps to ensure that the presence of the firearm is undetectable to casual (or trained) observers. Guns are usually secured in a holster specifically designed to aid concealment underneath everyday clothing.

Author Bio

Eileen S. ("Chick") Morgan, PhD, is a writer, singer songwriter, cabaret performer, podcast host, radio host, and arts entrepreneur. After a full career working globally with large companies and non-profits in leadership, strategy development, and execution, Chick now uses those skills as an arts entrepreneur, producing such experiences as Wimberley Alive! Arts and Music Festival; creating the inaugural Wimberley Storytelling Fest; and as Co-Visionary and Founder of Descanso Creatives International Writers' Retreats. Chick is also the Co-Founder of Wimberley Area Writers Group.

Everything's a Two-Step but a Waltz: The Reluctant Texan Comes Home is Chick's third book and first memoir. She lives outside of Austin, Texas in the Hill Country town of Wimberley with her fiancé, Robert Smith, and their excellent canine companions, Chase and Najee.

Eileen S. ("Chick") Morgan, PhD
morganphdiva@icloud.com
www.chickmorgan.com
You Tube: Morganphdiva
    and Wimberley Women With Standards
Spotify: Texas Chick

Reluctant Texan

Spotify Playlist
Enjoy the Music

MEZCALITA
PRESS

An independent publishing company
dedicated to bringing the printed poetry,
fiction, and non-fiction of musicians who
want to add to the power and reach
of their important voices.